The Althouse Press
Faculty of Education, The University of Western Ontario
Downey, THE FIFTY FATAL FLAWS OF ESSAY WRITING

THE FIFTY FATAL FLAWS

of Essay Writing

Glen R. Downey

The Althouse Press

First published in Canada in 2002 by
THE ALTHOUSE PRESS
Dean: *Allen Pearson*
Director of Publications: *Greg Dickinson*
Faculty of Education, The University of Western Ontario
1137 Western Road, London, Ontario, Canada N6G 1G7

Second printing: December 2002
Third printing: August 2003
Fourth printing: October 2004

Editorial Assistants: *Katherine Butson, Lois Armstrong, Jessie Coffey*
Cover design: *Lois Armstrong*

National Library of Canada Cataloguing in Publication

Downey, Glen R., 1969-
    The fifty fatal flaws of essay writing / Glen R. Downey

ISBN 0-920354-51-3

    1. Essay-Authorship.   2. English Language-Rhetoric.   I. Title

PE1471.D69 2002   808'.042'0711   C2002-902863-9

Printed and bound in Canada by Aylmer Express Ltd., 390 Talbot Street, E., Alymer, Ontario, Canada, N5H 2R9.

Contents

The Fifty Fatal Flaws of Essay Writing: An *Introduction*

The primary goal of this work is to help college and university students improve their essay writing. In each section, a problem frequently found in undergraduate papers is introduced, a solution is proposed, and, in most cases, a practical tip or exercise is given to help students eliminate the problem from their writing.

The sections are arranged in reverse numerical order, beginning with "50. The It's/Its Error" and ending with "1. Plagiarism." This is not to suggest that the problems discussed in the higher-numbered sections occur less frequently or are less problematic, but there is a general movement towards more serious errors (errors that by themselves can deprive a paper of a passing grade) as we count down from 50 to 1.

The Fifty Fatal Flaws of Essay Writing is not meant to replace other essay-writing handbooks but to complement them. It does not cover every conceivable grammatical, stylistic, or aesthetic error that might appear in an essay, nor does it make such an attempt. Instead, it chooses fifty common problems that occur in student essays and gives an overview of each of these problems by looking at a practical example.

One of the common complaints of first-year composition students is that they are judged so critically on mechanics but do not feel that they have been properly taught how to avoid these types of errors. However, a course in essay writing assumes that the student has a command, and not simply a basic understanding, of grammar. Thus, we arrive at an impasse; the professor's desire to teach writing at the *essay* level is waged against the student's desire to improve his or her writing at the *sentence* and *paragraph* levels. This work attempts to bridge these two agendas by (1) showing students how sentence and paragraph-level errors directly impact the grades they receive on their papers, and (2) giving students tips and exercises to help them improve their writing on all levels.

You will notice that some of the sections deal with problems that you may have never thought were problems, such as "46. Inappropriate Font" and "39. The Dreaded Opening Phrase: 'In today's society…'." When submitting an essay, however, we have to take advantage of every conceivable grammatical, stylistic, and *aesthetic* improvement if we want to guarantee ourselves the opportunity of securing a top mark. Generally, content is more important than presentation, but *The Fifty Fatal Flaws* tries to show that these two things are much more dependent on one another than we might have initially thought.

I hope that by having these common writing problems presented to them in a compact and easy-to-follow format, students will not be intimidated about having to read lengthy sections of prose in order to understand some of the difficulties they are having with their writing. In addition, I welcome suggestions about this handbook and encourage students to read its prose critically so that their detective work might uncover those moments where I myself use the odd contraction or split the occasional infinitive. Happy hunting!

50. *The It's/Its Error*

The Problem: | The worst thing about this CD is **it's** lack of originality.

Even experienced writers encounter difficulty with this basic grammatical error, but if you are taking a composition course with an instructor who likes nothing better than to stay up all night looking for **it's/its** errors, you simply cannot afford to make this mechanical mistake. The reason we get this wrong so often is that when we are talking about something that someone *owns* we use an **'s** to indicate possession:

| The band**'s** creativity has dwindled a bit recently.

So, when we have to make a decision about whether to use **it's** or **its** for the possessive case, we often make the mistake of thinking that we should use the one that *looks* like a possessive: **it's**. Now this would be absolutely splendid if it were not incorrect, but unfortunately, **its** and not **it's** is used to indicate a possessive; it just happens to be backwards, that's all.

The Solution: | The worst thing about this CD is **its** lack of originality.

The way to correct **it's/its** errors is to use the following trick: every time you encounter either **it's** or **its** in your writing, ask yourself the following question:

Am I really trying to say **it is**?

If you are trying to say **it is** then you should be using **it's**. This is easy to remember if you think about the apostrophe in **it's** as the dot of the missing "i":

I t **'** s
I t **i** s

Practical Exercise:

Find an article in either a magazine or a newspaper and go through it, cir-cling each and every *it's* or *its* that you come across. When you have circled all of them, go to the first one and ask yourself the question: *Is the writer really try-ing to say "it is"?*

If the answer is yes, then the writer should have an *it's* rather than an *its*. Try to see if you can find five instances in which writers have incorrectly used *its* instead of *it's* or vice versa. You can begin with my M.A. thesis.

49. Incorrect (Parenthetical) References

The Problem:

> As Annie Dillard suggests, "People take vows of poverty, chastity, and obedience—even of silence—by choice." **(Dillard, p. 52)**

Documentation errors drive professors crazy, but not because they really care whether or not it is appropriate in a reference to (1) use a "p." to indicate that what follows is a page number, or (2) include the author's name in the reference if the person has already been mentioned in the sentence, or (3) put the sentence-ending period in the wrong place. No, professors are driven crazy because they were all taught how to document correctly, and every time they see something being documented incorrectly it catches their eye, even for a split second, and distracts them from what they are reading. They react with an unspoken, "Hmm, that's not right," and before you know it they're thinking about whether they will have to make a note in your text about MLA (*Modern Language Association*) format, whether they will have to correct the error every time it appears in the essay, and whether they will have to deduct marks for incorrect documentation. Perhaps by this point, they have even forgotten what your argument is.

The Solution:

> As Annie Dillard suggests, "People take vows of poverty, chastity, and obedience—even of silence—by choice" (52).

The MLA rules of style aim at simplicity, and 99% of the time the student makes a documentation error by putting too much information in the parenthetical reference rather than not enough. Typically, a parenthetical reference contains the last name of the author and the page number from which the quote was taken. In the above example, we need to include only the page number since the author, Dillard, is mentioned in the sentence.

A wise investment for anyone interested in pursuing an academic career in the humanities is the *MLA Handbook for Writers of Research Papers* (5th ed.) by Joseph Gibaldi. This work covers in-text parenthetical references as well as how to list references in a bibliography. If you are having to cite a book by multiple authors, an article in an online periodical, an unpublished dissertation, or a personal interview, the *MLA Handbook* has detailed instructions about how to document all of these sources.

It should be noted that MLA is the documentation style of choice for humanities disciplines—and more specifically, English—while APA (*American Psychological Association*) style tends to be given preference in psychology and the social sciences. In addition, the University of Chicago style is sometimes used in those subjects where a footnote or endnote style is preferred. An excellent resource for those interested in how to document both print and non-print sources in each of these styles is Joanne Buckley's *Fit to Print: The Canadian Student's Guide to Essay Writing*, 4th ed. (1998).

Practical Exercise:

Imagine that you are an editor who has been asked to convert the documentation of a scholarly essay into MLA format. Find an older (pre-1970) article that uses footnotes or some other referencing format and determine how it should be changed to conform to the MLA rules of style.

48. The Comma Splice

The Problem:

> I spent my first year of university studying the natural sciences, in the summer I took a literature course.

The comma splice is a serious grammatical error that occurs when a writer attempts to join two sentences with a comma. The above non-sentence is grammatically incorrect because the writer has taken two independent statements that can stand alone as sentences ("I spent my first year of university studying the natural sciences" and "in the summer I took a literature course") and stuck them together with a comma. Without the comma the sentence is a run-on (a mechanical problem that most students know they are supposed to avoid), but with the comma we still have a grammatical error. The writer is missing a coordinating conjunction: a word that can conjoin the two statements to make them one.

The Solution:

> I spent my first year of university studying the natural sciences, **but** in the summer I took a literature course.

The above statement is now a grammatically correct sentence. The coordinating conjunction "but" links both halves of the sentence together by indicating that the content of the second part contrasts with the content of the first. Another way to eliminate the comma splice is to replace the comma with a semi-colon:

> I spent my first year of university studying the natural sciences; in the summer I took a literature course.

Fifty Fatal Flaws

Practical Exercise:

How would you correct the following comma splice errors by incorporating conjunctions?

1. The driver does not know how to get there, he cannot remember the way.

2. I could not stop for death, it kindly stopped for me.

3. That student goes to parties, he never fails to come home drunk.

4. I agree with you, I happen to think Marx was a genius.

5. Candy is dandy, however, liquor is quicker.

As you read through these sentences, you might begin to recognize that using different conjunctions in a given sentence can substantially change what is being said.

Note: Examples of solutions to this and other practical exercises can be found at the end of this book.

47. *The Comma Error*

The Problem: | Leaving the party early, was difficult for Fred to do. |

The comma error is a grammatical error that occurs when a writer divides the subject of a sentence from its verb with a comma. In the above sentence, a comma separates the subject "Leaving" from its verb "was." Although most students would not write "Leaving, was difficult," the use of longer and more complex subjects can result in comma errors when the writer feels as though he or she has come to a natural pause in the sentence (watch out especially for sentences that begin with an infinitive). I am not trying to suggest that commas will never come between a subject and its verb, but in such a case you need to have a pair of commas that are setting apart an insertion.

The Solution: | Leaving the party early, **however,** was difficult for Fred to do. |

In this second sentence, the subject and its verb are separated by commas, but there is no comma error. The word, "however," is functioning as an interjection and is indicating that the information in this sentence contrasts with what has just come before. Often a parenthetical or "non-restrictive" clause will come between a subject and its verb without forming a comma error.

Practical Exercise:

Examine the sentences below and determine which have comma errors:

1. Sylvester, the lovable but hopeless cartoon cat, is always trying to devour Tweety.

2. Being upset and disoriented after the accident, was the reason the driver fled the scene.

3. The way to open a present, is not with caution and reserve, but with reckless abandon.

4. Only when things calmed down and eventually returned to order, did he decide that it was eventually time to be going.

5. Watching the World Series is, without a doubt, one of the most pleasant ways to spend an October afternoon.

When you are looking at the above sentences, try to figure out which ones have interjections, which ones have non-restrictive clauses that describe the subject, and which ones have comma errors.

46. *Inappropriate Font*

The Problem:

> **Early myths concerning the origins of chess were devised in an effort to validate the hierarchical nature of medieval society and to discourage those who would question it.**

You may be wondering why I would make an issue out of choosing an inappropriate font. "The font I use in typing up my essay should have no bearing on the grade I receive!" you might exclaim, and yet, in truth, there is nothing more annoying for a professor than to turn to the first page of an essay and see a text that uses a ten-point, *sans serif* font and is one-and-a-half, rather than double, spaced. A professor will often take your paper and shove it to the bottom of the pile so that he or she can delay dealing with the annoyance of going through the essay.

The Solution:

> Early myths concerning the origins of chess were devised in an effort to validate the hierarchical nature of medieval society and to discourage those who would question it.

Whenever you submit a formal essay, always use twelve-point Times New Roman, Courier, or a similar *serif* font. Fonts with serifs are those that have the little tails on the tops and bottoms of the letters, just as this Goudy font that I am using right now does. *Sans serif* fonts, like Swiss, Helvetica, or Arial, have no tails and consequently make it more difficult for your eye to follow them across the page. The little serifs act as encouraging visual guides, and without these a *sans serif* font arrests your gaze. Thus, you should always use a *serif* font for text and a *sans serif* font only for titles and headings—the former makes for easy reading and the latter draws visual attention to important information.

Practical Exercise:

Take a couple of old essays (three or four pages in length would be appropriate) that you have saved on your word processor and print them out. Then change the font of the essays from twelve point to ten point and from *serif* to *sans serif*. With the first pair of essays read the twelve-point, *serif* text first and then the ten-point, *sans serif* text. Time how long it takes to read each of these. For the second pair of essays, go in reverse order.

You should find that it takes significantly longer to read a ten-point *sans serif* text. The problem with this is that the longer it takes the professor to read a paper, the greater the chance that he or she will think there must be something wrong *with the content of the text* and not just with the format.

45. Jargon and Other Obfuscatory Practices

The Problem: In consecrating the taxonomic potential of binary opposit-ions, the patriarchal hegemony endeavours to quell its own Freudian anxieties regarding gender difference.

I could repeat this sentence to an audience of feminist critical theorists and they might say, "Yeah, tell me something I don't know!" However, if I were to say it to a gathering of family relatives during the Christmas holidays, reactions would be quite different: "Poor Glen, he's working much too hard in Oakville," or "Did he just make fun of us?" In either case, however, the sentence contains an unacceptable level of *jargon*, words that have very specialized meanings and that should be used sparingly.

In Lewis Carroll's *Through the Looking-Glass*, Humpty Dumpty tells Alice that "words mean just what I tell them to mean, no more, no less," but Alice is not convinced. Humpty forgets that it takes two people to agree on whether a definition is truthful or accurate. A scholarly essay is written to communicate ideas, but if the writer is the only person who can understand what the paper says, then he or she has failed to communicate.

The Solution: Men unfairly put women into categories in an effort to feel better about themselves.

Often we think that using the most complex language possible will impress our professors and make them sit up and take notice. Well, they do sit up and take notice when they read a sentence littered with jargon, but it's not the kind of notice that we are looking for. You should always strive to use simple words to communicate complex ideas rather than use complex words to communicate simple ideas. Remember, simple language does not have to consist of a series of monosyllabic words, and there is an important distinction between what is *simple* to understand (good) and what is *simplistic* (bad).

Practical Exercise:

Find a newspaper article on a subject with which you are only marginally familiar. Read through the article and every time you come to a word that you do not understand, or that appears to be jargon, underline it and then look it up in the dictionary and try to find a simpler synonym. Determine whether the article meets its objective of communicating with a wide public audience, and if it does not, write a letter to the editor in clear and simple prose that takes issue with the degree of jargon in the article in question.

44. Speling Mistaks

The Problem:
> It is important to make a concerted effort not to **mispell** words in an essay.

Students will often demonstrate an ability to adhere to all of the strict principles of writing a coherent essay except the one that reads: "Thou shalt not misspell." In general, professors have mixed feelings about this problem; although they all agree that students should be able to spell, some are much more lenient than others when it comes to deducting marks for spelling mistakes on in-class and take-home essays. However, the general consensus is that while all words in a paper should be spelled correctly, misspelling fairly complex words in an in-class essay is occasionally forgivable. All other instances of misspelling, however, are not acceptable.

The Solution:
> It is important to make a concerted effort not to **misspell** words in an essay.

There are a number of excellent strategies that writers can use to improve their spelling. The first one, you will not be surprised to discover, is to read as much as you can. When you see words being consistently spelled correctly, you will begin to spell them correctly yourself. The second strategy is to do something which you may initially think is unusual: *read your essays backwards*. When we typically read something we do not do it one word at a time; our eyes scan several words at once and in so doing they occasionally miss spelling mistakes. When we read an essay backwards, however, we cannot make sense of the text because it is not being read in the correct order. Thus, our eyes concentrate on each individual word rather than scanning groups of words at once.

Also, don't accept every correction that a spellchecker makes because spellcheckers are notorious for making poor suggestions (for instance, when they do not recognize a word like *Canadians* and insist that you use *Canadian* instead). Avoid proofreading the final draft of your essay while it is still on your computer screen. Our eyes seem to do much better in looking at a hard copy of a text.

Practical Exercise:

Get a newspaper article and read through it, trying to understand what is being said but also looking for any spelling mistakes (typically, we do both of these activities in proofreading our own essays). When you have done this, try reading the article backwards to see if you can spot some mistakes that you did not notice on your first reading. Another practical exercise is to take an old essay that you have saved and run it through the spell checker. How many times does the spellchecker make a valid suggestion and how many times does it make one that is inappropriate?

Once you have done these exercises, have a go at the following spelling test. It seems very reasonable, since the correct choices are just sitting there waiting to be circled, but don't be surprised if you are able to get only half of these right. We use a number of words in our everyday speech that we very seldom write down.

"Tricky Diction"

For each of the twenty-five groups of words below indicate the word that is spelled correctly by circling it.

1.	mispelled	misspelled	misspeled
2.	ecstacy	exstacy	ecstasy
3.	cemetary	cematery	cemetery
4.	irresistable	irresistible	irrisestible
5.	medieval	medeival	mediavel
6.	auxilliary	auxiliary	auxillary
7.	erroneous	eroneous	erroneus
8.	villian	villan	villain
9.	possession	posession	possesion

10. separate   seperate   separete

11. paralell   parralell   parallel

12. neccessary   neccesary   necessary

13. minuscule   miniscule   minescule

14. primative   primiteve   primitive

15. souvenier   souveneer   souvenir

16. refering   reffering   referring

17. recommend   recomend   reccomend

18. secretary   secratary   secratery

19. disasterous   disastrous   disasterious

20. benefitted   benifitted   benefited

21. attendent   attendant   atendant

22. conceivable   concievable   conceivible

23. independant   independant   independent

24. fictitious   fictitous   fictious

25. criticism   critisism   critcism

43. *The Poor Title*

The Problem:

> **HAMLET**
> by Joe Student
> English 100

Oh, how many times have I eagerly gathered up my first batch of essays for the semester, brought them to the peace and quiet of my office for an afternoon of marking, only to turn to the first paper and see the above title? "Good God," I say to myself, "doesn't he know that *that* title has already been taken? It's Shakespeare's, not his, for heaven's sake!" Of course, I eventually calm down, pull out my trusty pen, circle the title, and then write a comment like: "You need to have a more original title." The reason students often omit a creative title is that their title page is left until the morning that their paper is due. "Title, hmm, yeah title...the prof said I had to have one so...um...yeah, Hamlet!" "Hamlet" tells me what work of literature the paper is examining, but it is an inappropriate title for an essay *about Hamlet*. However, it is at least marginally superior to that much more dreaded visitor of first-year composition title pages: *Essay #1*.

The Solution:

> "Mad in Craft": Madness and Roleplaying in William
> Shakespeare's *Hamlet*
> by Joe Student
> English 100

Often, a good idea is to use a two-part title divided by a colon. In the example above, the student gives a quote from the play in the first part of his title and then uses the second part to describe very accurately the subject of his essay. When the professor reads the student's title page, he or she immediately understands what the paper is about and looks forward to reading it. On the other hand, the ambiguous "Hamlet" does not tell the professor anything, except that the paper has something to do with Shakespeare's play, and it suggests that the writer *has not taken time and care in preparing the essay.*

Practical Exercise:

Select an article either from the newspaper or a scholarly journal, but avoid looking at the title. Once you have finished reading the article, decide on an appropriate title and jot down a few reasons why you have made your choice. Then look at the title of the article and examine what similarities and differences are to be found in the article's given title and the one you have chosen. Which do you feel is more appropriate, and why?

42. The Dangling Modifier

The Problem:
> Previously concealed by a sliding panel, the hero found a secret passage.

Every writer on the planet makes this grammatical error from time to time. We begin a sentence with a dependent clause, put our comma down, but then forget about the person or thing to which the dependent clause is referring. The problem with the above sentence is that in its present form it suggests that "the hero" was "previously concealed by a sliding panel," but you and I both know that the writer probably meant that the "secret passage," and not the hero, was the thing being concealed. At the very least, we are confused about what was covering what or whom, and this is not the sort of thing that you want a professor fiddling over when he or she is supposed to be appreciating the fine argument you are making in your essay.

The Solution:
> The hero found a secret passage **that was previously concealed by a sliding panel.**

Usually, dangling modifiers can be rectified by putting the descriptive, dependent clause in close proximity to the person or thing that it is describing. In the above example, we can simply rearrange the sentence to make it perfectly clear what was being concealed. This is better than leaving the sentence as is and using a passive construction: "Previously concealed by a sliding panel, the secret passage was found by the hero."

Practical Exercise:

Analyze the following sentences and indicate which ones have dangling modifiers and which ones do not. Explain how each dangling modifier you find makes it difficult for readers to piece together the meaning of the particular sentence in question.

1. Returning from his trip overseas, the house was as deserted as Peter had left it.

2. Acknowledging some mistakes in its recent article, a correction was printed by the local newspaper.

3. Indebted to the members of the committee for all their help, Elizabeth bought them each a bottle of *Dom Perignon*.

4. Pleased that the weather was gradually improving, the spring fashion line could be introduced by the company without any fear of poor sales.

41. Non Sequiturs

The Problem: | Imposing stiffer fines and longer jail sentences for the possession of illegal narcotics will prevent heroin addicts from remaining addicted.

The term *non sequitur* is a Latin expression meaning "it does not follow." This logical error occurs when the conclusions we draw are not supported by the evidence we present. In the above example, the writer seems to be making a fairly reasonable argument: that if you punish heroin addicts by fining and incarcerating them you will deprive them of the means to continue taking the drug. However, heroin addiction is based on the body's physical dependency on specific chemicals in the drug, and although putting users in jail and fining them might temporarily prevent them from obtaining access to heroin, it by no means follows that this *will prevent heroin addicts from remaining addicted.* Drug addicts have an amazing resourcefulness for coming up with the funds to support their habit (so imposing stiffer fines will not necessarily help) and drug use in prison is by no means uncommon (so imposing longer jail sentences is likely not the answer either).

The Solution: | Although imposing stiffer fines and longer jail sentences for the possession of illegal narcotics may pose some problems for heroin addicts, only education and treatment can help addicts overcome their addiction.

The way to eliminate *non sequitur* errors is to make sure that your evidence supports the conclusions you draw from it. Look carefully at those moments in your essay where you appear to be making a very confident pronouncement, and make sure that you have provided sufficient evidence to support your claims.

Do not be at all surprised if you come across a couple of *non sequiturs* in a current or past essay. In our postmodern age, it is often difficult for us to avoid making this type of logical error because we are so inundated with visual *non sequiturs* from both the media and the world of advertising.

Practical Exercise:

The next time you are watching television, try to see how many *non sequiturs* you can spot during a typical commercial. An example that comes to mind is an old ad for wrinkle-free pants, in which a gorgeous woman is ready to throw herself at a guy who does not need to iron his creaseless pants. This tells the consumer: "If you buy wrinkle-free pants, sexy women will beat a path to your door." Although it does not follow that wearing wrinkle-free pants equals instant popularity (or will in any way improve your sex life), this type of commercial tends to be quite effective.

40. Dead Metaphors

The Problem:

> The remarkable ambience inside the restaurant shows that **you can't judge a book by its cover.**

A "dead metaphor" is a metaphor whose original significance has been lost over the centuries—it was once alive, but we have systematically killed it through overuse. Indeed, the metaphor has become so common that we use it without really scrutinizing whether or not it is even appropriate. In the above excerpt from an essay reviewing a local restaurant, the student is attempting to capture the difference between what the restaurant looks like on the outside and the atmosphere of the place once you go inside. However, in using the dead metaphor to describe the restaurant's ambience, the student prevents the reader from fully appreciating what it must be like to dine at the restaurant. The cliché sticks in the reader's mind and he or she might even get the idea that the restaurant's ambience is cliché, that it is as dead as the metaphor which describes it.

The Solution:

> The remarkable ambience inside the restaurant shows that the building's homely exterior is altogether misleading.

Dead metaphors should never be resurrected for any reason; it's best just to say what you mean, making your point as clear and concise as possible. In the above example, the student is trying to convey how the building's exterior does not give a proper indication of how nice the restaurant is inside, and so she has taken out the dead metaphor and replaced it with a very unambiguous statement of what she means.

Practical Exercise

For each of the dead metaphors or clichés given below, figure out what it means and then use it in a sentence. Once you have written the sentence, try to rewrite it by removing the dead metaphor and replacing it with a clearer and more concise statement of what you mean.

1. tight as a drum
2. avoid like the plague
3. face the music
4. cool as a cucumber
5. last but not least
6. happy as a clam
7. slowly but surely
8. a night to remember
9. the world is your oyster

39. The Dreaded Opening Phrase: "In today's society"

The Problem:

> In today's society, body piercing and tattooing have become common cultural practices.

Just as a poor title will give your professor fits before he or she even gets to the argument of your essay, so will the dreaded opening phrase, "In today's society." The problem with the expression is that it does not really mean anything. Now, most professors understand that "today" does not necessarily denote "this very day," but can connote an unspecified but fairly current period of time. And generally, professors also understand what is meant by "society": people gathered together for presumably a common purpose and having their own distinctive cultural patterns and institutions. However, the problem comes about when these two terms are thrown together: when we say "today's society," what do we really mean? Do we mean the society of the British Columbia lower mainland region (as opposed to Vancouver Island), or do we mean South American society (Rio, Caracas, or La Paz?), or do we mean the society of central Tibet? In the example given above, we can see that the sentence may or may not be true depending on whether we are talking about people from Toronto, or from Baghdad, or from Capetown.

The Solution:

> Recently, body piercing and tattooing have become common cultural practices in many parts of Canada and the United States.

The way to eliminate an ambiguous phrase like "In today's society" is to be specific about precisely what group of people you are referring to. No professor is going to take issue with your contention that body piercing and tattooing have recently become popular forms of body modification in North America, but he or she might take issue with an ambiguous expression that seems to refer both to everyone and to no one.

Practical Exercise:

For this exercise you should take a look at a magazine article, an Internet web page, and perhaps one of your old essays. Try to find instances in which either you or other writers have made a significant assumption about who or what is being referred to in a specific phrase or sentence. Check to see how many times the word "society" is referred to in a particular piece of writing, and determine whether it is used correctly or forms an inappropriate generalization. You may want to consult with your professor to see if he or she has the same reaction.

38. The Succession of Short Sentences

The Problem:
> Restaurants should be smoke-free environments. Second-hand smoke is very dangerous. Non-smoking patrons breathe it in and get sick. It's just not fair.

One thing that you always want to avoid when you are writing is the construction of monotonous sentences, large ponderous beasts packed with a host of meaningless adjectives and adverbs. However, monotony for the reader is also created when the writer strings together a series of short sentences. In the above example, the writer is telling us some important information, but his succession of short sentences makes what he says seem choppy and almost child-like. It reminds us of the *Fun with Dick and Jane* books that we read when we were kids. This is not to suggest that short sentences are always ineffective, but the grouping together of a number of them is usually a stylistic mistake.

The Solution:
> Restaurants should be smoke-free environments, because patrons should not be forced to breathe in toxins.

There is a point at which concise writing becomes too concise, when sentence after sentence consists of only a handful of words. Ironically, however, a succession of short sentences, which seems to strive at conciseness of expression, often has the opposite result. By putting two or three sentences into one we eliminate a lot of the extra words that we need in forming each individual sentence. Of the two examples given above, the first is eight words longer than the second (counting hyphenated compounds as one word) and contains three more conjugated verbs. Using the extra space that the corrected version frees up, the writer can include additional material to support his argument.

Practical Exercise:

For each of the following, take the succession of short sentences and form one or more complex or compound sentences.

1. Cyclists often ride in between cars. This is dangerous. A bicycle is still a vehicle. It should behave like a vehicle. There's no reason why cyclists should do this.

2. Managing our forests is important. Clear-cutting decimates entire sections of forest. We need responsible forest management. This means that we'll all have to do our share.

3. Reading is one of the best activities. It's easy to do and relaxing. You can lose yourself in a story. When you read, you learn a lot and have fun at the same time.

37. *Grammatically Awkward Lists*

The Problem:

> When asked about ways to improve our health and fitness, doctors recommend exercise, **having** a good diet, plenty of sleep, and **to get** regular check-ups.

Awkwardness in one's writing is often difficult to correct, especially when a professor simply underlines our sentences and writes something like, "This is rather awkward." "Sure it's awkward," you might say when you get the paper back and read it over, "but that doesn't really tell me how to correct the problem!" Usually, a professor will make a correction if he or she can easily fix the sentence, but sometimes the sentence is awkward for a reason that cannot be immediately determined. For professors, one of those awkwardnesses (that seems to fall somewhere in between the "easily correctable" and the "I'll just put 'Awkward' and hope the student figures out that something is wrong...") is the grammatically awkward list. Sometimes this error is easily correctable and sometimes a great deal of care and patience is needed in order to fix the problem.

Whenever you list items, they should be *grammatically parallel*: they should each begin with the same part of speech, whether this be a noun, or an infinitive, or a gerund, or whatever. When different items in a list represent different parts of speech, the reader finds it difficult to make sense of what is being itemized. In the example above, the first item in the list is a noun, "exercise"; the second item begins with the gerund "having"; the third begins with the noun, "plenty," which is quantifying "sleep"; and the fourth begins with the infinitive "to get." The sentence, as is, reads very awkwardly.

The Solution:

> When asked about ways to improve our health and fitness, doctors recommend exercise, good eating habits, plenty of sleep, and regular check-ups.

With just a few minor changes we are able to take a grammatically awkward list and turn it into something that the reader has very little trouble processing. Yes, the second and fourth items begin with adjectives instead of nouns, but these adjectives are by no means distracting and are, in fact, necessary for our successful comprehension of the sentence.

Practical Exercise:

Find a piece of writing that contains a number of lists—a description of a procedure is a good one, and you might even think about trying certain sections of a cookbook—and see how many grammatically awkward lists you can find in twenty minutes. Once you have underlined the lists, determine how you would correct them in order to make them grammatically parallel. Once you have done this, check for examples from your own writing, looking closely at previous essays.

36. The Single-Source Research Paper

The Problem:

> Henry James's literary criticism is an important adjunct to his fiction (Merrill 379): "Much of his criticism is contained in informal reviews collected in a *Library of America* edition" (379). In these reviews, James gives a number of insights into the intellectual milieu of his time (379).

Sometimes when we have to write a research paper we make the rather poor decision to leave it until the last minute. But we do not simply leave our *writing* of it to the last minute; we leave our *thinking* about it as well. In a mad scramble to get our paper in to the professor, we forget about thinking for ourselves and instead decide to pay a visit to the library. Of course, many of our classmates are also writing on the same subject and they have managed to take out every book but one. "Well, no problem," we think, "I'm sure this critic has plenty of interesting things to say...." However, a research paper is not supposed to represent your understanding of one particular critic's opinion (unless this is the assigned topic), but how your own ideas and opinions can be situated within a pre-existing framework of critical research created by many different scholars with many different perspectives. If, as in the case above, I simply rely on Merrill's interpretation of James' literary career, I would be missing out on the opinions of Joseph Beach, Sarah Daugherty, Leon Edel, and others who have written on James.

The Solution:

> Henry James's literary criticism is an important adjunct to his fiction, especially his informal reviews collected in the *Library of America* edition which give a number of crucial insights into the intellectual milieu of his time (Merrill 379). James's proficiency in writing both fiction and non-fiction encourages us to see how versatile certain writers are in being able to master the techniques of very different genres. As Joseph Beach has noted...

Fifty Fatal Flaws

Here, we have condensed Merrill's observations and followed them with our own. We are now expressing what the critic has prompted us to think about, and this is precisely what a professor reading our paper wants to see.

Practical Tip:

When you read a scholarly source, ask yourself if you agree with what the critic has said. We often think that library books are written by god-like figures who are never wrong, but if they were never wrong, why would people still need to be writing books?

35. The S p l i t Infinitive

The Problem:

> The defendant followed his lawyer's recommendation **to categorically deny** the charges.

Those of you who excitedly follow the latest developments in the world of acceptable grammar usage will already know that split infinitives have crept their way back into the realm of the acceptable. However, while *you* may know this, your professor may not, and won't *you* look like Mr. or Ms. Smarty Pants trying to convince the instructor that the correction on your paper should not really be there.

Despite the fact that we are now able "to boldly go" splitting our infinitives with reckless abandon, we should be very careful when we do so. The two problems that arise with split infinitives are that (1) often the word that splits the infinitive does not really add much to the sentence, and (2) if more than one word splits the infinitive, this nearly always creates a stylistic awkwardness. The above sentence is an example of the first case. Why does the word "categorically" have to be in the sentence at all? Does it really make the "denying" that much more impressive?

An example of the second case (and also, incidentally, the first) might be the following: "He plotted to recklessly and with malice aforethought undertake a criminal enterprise." The preposition "to" and the verb "undertake" are so far apart that what comes in between them seems to spoil the sentence. Also, if someone is plotting to commit a crime, do we really need to stress the fact that the person is "reckless" and has "malice aforethought"?

The Solution:

> The defendant followed his lawyer's recommendation **to deny** the charges.

You do not need to eliminate adverbs from your writing, or avoid using them when constructing an infinitive; you just need to be smart about where you put them. Sometimes it sounds better to split an infinitive and sometimes it

41

doesn't. However, if you suspect that a split infinitive in your essay might be interpreted as awkward, you should play it safe and either eliminate the adverb or put it outside the infinitive.

Practical Tip:

To check for split infinitives in your essay, use the search function on your word processor to find every occurrence of "to" or "to_" ("to" followed by a space), and then quickly flip from hit to hit looking for *"to [adverb] [verb]"* constructions. You will, of course, come across a number of *to's* that are not the first part of an infinitive, but these can be ignored. The whole process should not take more than a couple of minutes.

34. When a Contraction's Inappropriate

The Problem:

> If **it's** inappropriate to use contractions in a formal essay, why **weren't** we told?

Some professors are terribly annoyed by this stylistic inaccuracy and others, quite frankly, could not care less. Once upon a time, I made a big deal about contractions in formal writing, telling students each time they received their papers back that at least half of them had used contractions and that this was not considered acceptable in their essays. Now, however, after years of being ignored (sigh), I tend to go after the more serious grammatical problems in a paper and only make a note about contraction use once or twice during the course of marking an essay.

Still, while contractions are perfectly acceptable in speech and in informal writing (for instance, in personal letters, emails, and chat rooms), they are perceived as unprofessional when they appear in a formal essay. If you are taking the time to craft an argument, the logic goes, why would you want to clutter it with words that sound like lazy speech. One could argue that contractions help to save space and to make one's argument more compact, but for the amount of space you would actually be getting, the trade off is just not worth it.

The Solution:

> If **it is** inappropriate to use contractions in a formal essay, why **were** we **not** told?

Sometimes it will seem awkward not to use a contraction in a particular instance when you are writing an essay. If avoiding the contraction seems to create an awkwardness, you can often reword that part of the sentence to get around the problem. Remember, though, if you are quoting a critical source or a passage from a work of poetry or fiction you must transcribe word-for-word the passage in question, even if it contains a significant number of contractions.

Practical Tip:

If you are a chronic contractions-user and your professor has a problem with this, there is a simple trick you can use to eliminate them from your writing. Just as using the search function to find all occurrences of "to" or "to_" helps us check for split infinitives, using it to find all occurrences of apostrophes will help us eliminate contractions. Again, you can go through an entire essay checking for contractions in a matter of minutes.

33. Ending (or Not Ending) a Sentence with a Preposition

The Problem:

> Being unemployed is a very difficult position to find oneself in.

Like the split infinitive (and to some extent, like the contraction), the sentence-ending preposition will elicit from your professor anything from a "Hmm" to a "No, no, NO!" (I happen to be more of a "Hmm" person myself). In most cases, you should probably avoid ending a sentence with a preposition even though it is technically not a grammatical error. However, you should not avoid ending a sentence with a preposition if to do so creates an awkwardness. You might say, "That is something I will not put up with" but you would not catch anyone saying: "That is something *up with which I will not put.*"

The Solution:

> Being unemployed is a very difficult position **in which** to find oneself.

You might be looking at the above correction and thinking to yourself, "What's so wonderful about this new sentence. Come to think of it, I don't think it's any better than the first one." Nevertheless, if you have a sentence in your essay that ends in a preposition and it can be rearranged without creating an awkwardness, it probably should be. However, if you cannot eliminate the sentence-ending preposition without creating a decidedly confusing grammatical construction, you should retain your original sentence. Of course, you could attempt to reword the sentence entirely. In these situations, use your best judgment.

Practical Exercise:

Examine the following sentences and determine whether or not they should end with a preposition. Then examine how they could be rearranged to eliminate any awkwardness.

1. The old gorge was something that the authorities never expected anyone to fall into.

2. Hamilton is the city that I originally came from.

3. Without a doubt, that is the worst case of influenza I have ever heard of.

4. This is an awful predicament to be in!

5. Where is the office he worked at?

6. Computer fantasy role-playing games are just the sort of thing you can get hooked on.

32. Gender Specificity

The Problem:

> Our mission is to seek out new worlds and new civilizations—to boldly go where no **man** has gone before.

Many of you will recognize this from the old *Star Trek* series of the late sixties. It's read in a voice-over at the beginning of each show and briefly explains why Kirk, Spock, and the rest are blazing across the galaxy week in and week out. What you may not have noticed, however, is that it contains gender-specific language, using the noun "man" to refer to both men and women. Traditionally, we have made these assumptions in our culture and in our language: that the reader is a "man," that human beings are "men," and that men and women together collectively constitute "mankind."

The problem with doing this is that we are failing to acknowledge women as individuals; indeed, we are using sexist language to eliminate women from the very page on which we write. By lumping women and men together under the headings of "men" and "mankind," we deprive women of their individuality and identity.

The Solution:

> Our mission is to seek out new worlds and new civilizations—to boldly go where no **one** has gone before.

Those of you who are fans of *Star Trek: The Next Generation* (now in syndication) will no doubt recognize this modernized version of the gender-specific voice-over from the original series. As you can see, eliminating gender specific language is a fairly simple matter, although it does have a couple of tricks that you need to learn in order to avoid having a number of sentences that discuss what "he or she" did to "him or her." The best thing to do, and this can nearly always be accomplished, is to change the subject of your sentence to a plural and take advantage of the fact that the third-person plural is the gender-neutral *they*. Instead of having the ridiculously awkward sentence: "A professor gives his or her opinion to his or her student when he or she wants him or her to improve his or her writing," you can simply write, "Professors give their opinions to students when they want them to improve their writing."

Practical Exercise:

No matter how hard we try to eliminate gender specific language, we always find some creeping into our writing. Take a look at either a magazine or a newspaper article (or perhaps even better, an old scholarly essay), and try to find examples of gender specific language. Strictly as an exercise, write a letter to the individual pointing out the instances of sexist language in the article and how these sentences could be amended.

31. Clearly, Certainly, and Obviously (or, Making the Reader Feel Stupid)

The Problem: | Certainly, it is obvious that the depletion of ozone in our atmosphere is a serious concern.

I include the triple terror of "clearly," "certainly," and "obviously" on my list of the fifty fatal flaws of essay writing because I used to be such an addict of these seemingly strong words. When I was writing my doctoral dissertation, my supervisor noticed that I had a tendency in those moments when my argument was on the shakiest ground to begin a sentence with "Certainly..." or "It is clear that...". He then told me what a wise man once told him: "Whenever you begin a sentence with 'Certainly' or 'Clearly,' the bull-$@%# factor in the sentence increases by exactly one hundred percent."

This is invaluable advice; we often use expressions like "it is obvious that" when we ourselves don't find things all that obvious. In an effort to persuade the reader of something of which we are not completely convinced, we introduce strong words or expressions that threaten to alienate the reader, who may not yet be fully prepared to agree with us. If, in the opening paragraph of an essay on capital punishment, I say, "It is obvious that criminals convicted of first degree murder should be rehabilitated rather than put to death," the tone of my sentence might possibly offend a certain segment of my readership. How would a reader who has lost a close relative to a violent crime feel about my sentence?

The Solution: | The depletion of ozone in our atmosphere is a serious concern.

You see, you do not need to litter your writing with words and phrases claiming how "clear" and "obvious" everything is. If you have a solid, well organized, and well-written essay, your argument will take care of that for you.

Practical Exercise:

Always check for words like "clearly," "certainly," and "obviously" when you are proofreading the final draft of your essay. The search function is once again useful for this sort of exercise. Find an old essay that you have saved on your hard drive and check to see how many times these sorts of words and their attendant phrases appear in your writing (another popular one, by the way, is "Without a doubt..."). Once you have looked through one of your essays, try to find examples in professional articles where writers rely on these words. How often do you notice writers using these words at a point in their argument where they seem to need to convince themselves of something?

30. Tense Switching

The Problem:

> *Raiders of the Lost Ark* **began** with Harrison Ford's character, Indiana Jones, trying to retrieve a golden statue from hidden ruins. Alfred Molina **plays** one of his guides and **gave** a decent, albeit brief, performance. Molina's character **is** impaled on spikes after trying to steal the statue, but when Indy **got** it, it **is** taken away from him by his arch rival.

Tense switching is a serious grammatical problem that plagues a number of writers. The most important thing with tense is being consistent, and so continually switching back and forth between the present and the past can prove deadly. We usually do not have a problem with tense when we are writing a personal narrative essay, but we often develop serious problems when we are writing a review of a book or a film. There is confusion because although we saw the film or read the book in the past, the events of the book or film happen in a kind of present—the present tense of the book or film.

However, what happens with the person who has not yet read the book or seen the film and is trying to decide whether or not it is something in which he or she is interested? The events of the book or film have not yet happened—indeed the story exists in the future, and yet he or she is reading a review of it in which the writer is moving back and forth between the present and the past. You can see how this generates confusion.

The Solution:

> *Raiders of the Lost Ark* **begins** with Harrison Ford's character, Indiana Jones, trying to retrieve a gold statue from hidden ruins. Alfred Molina **plays** one of his guides and **gives** a decent, albeit brief, performance. Molina's character **is** impaled on spikes after trying to steal the statue, but when Indy **gets** it, it **is** taken away from him by his arch rival.

Whenever you are discussing a work of literature, or a film, or a piece of art, always talk about it in the present tense. This eliminates any tense-switching problems and makes your discussion more immediate to the reader. You should use only the past tense when you are talking about an incident from the past or an historical event.

Practical Exercise:

Write a brief review of a film you have recently seen and pay careful attention to describing the events of the film in the present tense. When do you find yourself most tempted to switch to the past tense, and why do you think this is?

29. Usage Errors

The Problem: My appreciation of the film was negatively **effected** by all of the outlandish special **affects**.

    Usage errors typically have to be dealt with on a case by case basis. A writer might never confuse "to," "too," and "two" or "accept" and "except" but he or she might only be able to use "affect" and "effect" correctly seventy-five percent of the time. Sometimes we have strange gaps in our knowledge; I know someone who only recently discovered that the expression connoting a lacklustre effort is not, as they erroneously believed, "half-fast." Usage errors reflect our knowledge gaps by showing us that we occasionally do not recognize fundamental differences between closely sounding words. When I was young, I thought that the "Notary Public" was "The Nota Republic." And boy, did I want to go there!

The Solution: My appreciation of the film was negatively **affected** by all of the outlandish special **effects**.

    The way to avoid making the "effect/affect" usage error is to remember that "affect" is almost always a verb and "effect" is nearly always a noun. Following this rule, you'll probably be right ninety-nine times out of a hundred (except, of course, when you are talking about a certain *affect* or about *effecting* change, but these cases are rare).

    Sometimes usage is just a matter of consistency; for instance, do you know when it is correct to use "toward" and when it is correct to use "towards"? The answer is that they are the same and either can be used, but it is a stylistic mistake to switch back and forth between the two. You just have to choose one and be consistent. Most essay-writing handbooks contain a section that lists pairs of words which are commonly the victims of usage errors and it never hurts to go through these to familiarize yourself with the basic differences between similar sounding words.

Practical Exercise:

Listed below are pairs of words that are frequently confused in English. Distinguish between these terms by giving a brief explanation of their differences or by using them in sentences.

1. Allusion / Illusion
2. Ingenious / Genius
3. Rebut / Refute
4. Connotation / Denotation
5. Amoral / Immoral
6. Stationary / Stationery
7. Anxious / Eager
8. Elicit / Illicit
9. Censor / Censure

28. Inadequate Re(vision)

The Problem: In today's society, its okay to be yourself, in the past you had to **rigidly** conform. Everyone had to be **like peas in a pod**. What, was the fun in that?

Regardless of what you may have read, seen, or heard, revision is not the thing you do five minutes before you hand in a paper when you look at the fifth sentence in your opening paragraph and say: "Oh no, I spelled the Prime Minister's name wrong. Where's my liquid paper?!" Revision starts long before you get to class on your paper's due date. A professional writer will often spend only about half-an-hour writing a document and seven or eight hours making sure it is absolutely perfect. This is not an exaggeration. If you want to have a chance of getting a top mark on an essay, you need to put in several hours of revising, even for something as short as a three page paper. In the above passage, the writer has used the dreaded "In today's society" to open, and then has followed this with an "it's/its" error, a comma splice, a split infinitive, a dead metaphor, and finally a comma error.

The Solution: In contemporary western culture, it is okay to be yourself, whereas in the past you faced the miserable prospect of having to conform.

Even though college and university students often have a tremendous workload, a good policy is to finish your essay four or five days before it is due. Then you can let the paper sit for two days—you don't think about it, look at it, or worry about it. Now, when you put the paper away like this you have already started revising it. Indeed, you have spent considerable time proofreading it to make it as perfect as possible. However, when you come back to the paper two days later, you will be reading your paper with a fresh outlook—almost as though you are reading someone else's paper. Lo and behold, it's going to contain both stylistic and grammatical errors—it may even require additional content, or it might be too long. The point is that this second proofreading session can be used to find all of the mistakes that you failed to catch the first time around. When you leave your revising to the night before your paper is due, you are under pressure and do not really try to read all that closely. You sort of look at your paper out of one eye and say: "Yeah, hmm, that looks okay I think...I'll just be handing that in...."

Practical Exercise:

Get out an old essay that you did not do particularly well on and allow yourself a couple of hours to revise it. Try to find ten changes that you would make to the essay now that you have had an opportunity to look at it again after a significant period of time. Is there a pattern to be found in the things that you would change?

27. The Brutal Bibliography

The Problem:

> **BIBLIOGRAPHY**
>
> **1.** Huizinga, Johann, **Homo Ludens: A Study of the Play Element in Culture**. Boston: Beacon **Press**_ 1950.
>
> **2.** Berne, Eric, **Beyond Games and Scripts**. New York: Grove **Press, Inc._** 1976.

Although you might be able to get away with the above bibliography on the first couple of essays you submit for a first-year composition course, you cannot afford to use such a format for an MLA style research paper. The example above has a number of errors: (1) "Bibliography" should not be in block capitals, (2) The entries should not be numbered and each line should be double spaced, (3) The entries should be in alphabetical order, (4) Only the first line of each entry should be flush with the left margin; all succeeding lines should be indented, (5) The first name of each writer should be followed by a period and not a comma, (6) The titles of the books should either be in italics or underlined, (7) Words like "Press" and "Inc." should be omitted for conciseness, and (8) There should always be a comma between the place of publication and the publication date. Whew!

The Solution:

> Bibliography
>
> Berne, Eric. *Beyond Games and Scripts*. New York: Grove, 1976.
>
> Huizinga, Johann. *Homo Ludens: A Study of the Play Element in Culture*. Boston: Beacon, 1950.

Once again, the MLA rules of style aim at simplicity. The *MLA Handbook* contains rules for citing works from just about every medium conceivable, and it should always be consulted when you are unsure about how to prepare a particular bibliographical entry.

Practical Exercise:

Examine the bibliography below and determine which of its entries are acceptable and which are not. Circle anything that needs to be changed and explain your corrections in the space provided.

Bibliography

Allday Elizabeth. *Stefan Zweig: A Critical Biography* London, Allen, 1972

Beckett, Samuel. *Endgame,* New York City: Grove Press 1978.

Eliot, T. S. *Selected Poems.* London: Faber, 1971.

Eales. Richard, Chess: The History of a Game. London - Batsford, inc., 1985

Fisher, John. *The Magic Of Lewis Carroll,* London: Nelson, 1973.

Fine, Reuben. *"The Psychology of the Chess Player."* New York: Dover, 1967.

Keyes, Frances Parkinson. *The Chess Players.* New York: Farrar, 1960.

Levy David & Reuben, Stewart. The Chess Scene. London:Faber and Faber, 1974

Phillips, Robert, Ed. *Aspects of Alice.* NY: Vanguard Press, 1971.

Waitzkin, Fred, et al. <u>Searching for Bobby Fischer</u>. New York: Random, 1988.

26. Using "I believe that," "I think that," and "It is my opinion that"

The Problem: It is **my opinion that** drinking and driving is dangerous.

In a formal essay, you should always avoid using phrases like "I believe that," "It is my opinion that," or even worse, "I am personally of the belief that." Whenever you say something in your essay that does not end with a parenthetical reference attributing it to someone else, the reader assumes that what you have said is your opinion. When phrases like "I believe that" and "It is my opinion that" are used, they do not reinforce the extent to which you are convinced of these things so much as raise little flags in the reader's mind: "Why is this writer needing to tell me they *believe* this particular part of their argument? Are they unsure about something?"

You see, explicitly stating that you believe something or that it represents your opinion has the opposite of its intended effect. We use expressions like "I believe that" and "It is my opinion that" for emphasis, but in fact they produce a kind of negative emphasis and diminish the force of the particular statement that they modify.

The Solution: Drinking and driving is dangerous.

Our corrected sentence represents a one hundred percent improvement, and it gets much more quickly to the point than does the problem sentence, which is arguably misleading. Why is this first sentence misleading? Well, there is a general consensus among reasonable people that drinking and driving is dangerous. Thus, saying "It is my opinion that drinking and driving is dangerous" seems to carry with it the implication that *there are many other reasonable people who think drinking and driving is not dangerous.* This, however, is not really the case.

Practical Exercise:

Take a look at the following sentences and determine how you would correct them to make them more forceful.

1. I think the government can spy on us at will, and it is my opinion that this should stop.

2. I believe that by banning cellular telephones in cars, we can save lives.

3. It is my strong belief that the current economic forecast is erroneous.

4. I am personally of the belief that extraterrestrial life forms exist and are watching us.

25. The Argument of the Beard

The Problem: It is unfair to penalize drivers who have a blood/alcohol reading of .08 because it is impossible to tell at what point a person becomes drunk.

It is a logical fallacy to argue that because you cannot precisely define how many hairs it takes to make a beard, there is no distinction between someone with a beard and someone who is clean shaven. This is like saying that being drunk and sober are no different, or that night and day are the same, because you cannot tell when one becomes the other. The problem with this argument is that we know perfectly well when it is night and when it is day, and we can further define these periods as having certain characteristics (night is dark and usually cooler; day is light and usually warmer). The ancient Greek philosopher Zeno devised a number of logical paradoxes that are arguments of the beard. In one of these, he argued that you should not really be able to walk across a room because in order to do so, you would first have to walk half way across, and then half the distance from the half-way point, and then half of this distance...and so on forever. However, we know darn well that we *can* get across to that other side of the room. Zeno would have us believe that wherever we are standing, we are as near to or as far away from the opposite side as anyone else in the room. The refutation to the fallacy occurs, however, when we either have a knowledge of basic calculus, or when we say to Zeno: "Shut up and walk to the other side of the room, you annoying little man."

The Solution: It seems unfair that a driver can be fined for having a blood/alcohol reading of .08, and yet might be more capable of competently operating a motor vehicle than someone with a lower blood/alcohol reading.

I still do not happen to agree with this kind of argument, but at least it has an implicit point: intoxication depends both on physiology as well as on the

61

amount one has drunk. The problem with our initial sentence is that it makes the claim that "it is impossible to tell at what point a person becomes drunk." However, it *is* possible to tell at what point a person becomes drunk because there are certain characteristics that people under the influence of alcohol share, such as distorted perception, slurred speech, and diminished physical dexterity. Moreover, we have set a .08 blood/alcohol level as a guideline to define when someone is drunk, so it is fruitless to argue that it is impossible to tell.

Practical Tip:

Always be careful when you are attempting to suggest that there is no difference between two things that human beings traditionally consider to be very different. This is precisely the point at which an Argument of the Beard can creep into your essay.

24. Plot Summary

The Problem:

> Sometimes it is difficult to tell whether Hamlet is mad or whether he is feigning madness. **When Gertrude wishes to speak with her son, Polonius decides to hide behind the arras and listen to their conversation. Hamlet then arrives and starts berating his mother, whereupon Polonius cries out and Hamlet, thinking Polonius is Claudius, stabs him through the arras....**

Plot summary is the bane of the literary essay. When we have to write about a work of literature, we often think that by relating the events of the story we will, in fact, be arguing our case. In the above example, the student begins by suggesting that it is sometimes difficult to tell whether Hamlet is mad or only pretending to be mad in Shakespeare's play, but then falls into a mere recounting of the events of the story. A literary essay that consists primarily of plot summary will usually receive an F grade.

The Solution:

> Sometimes it is difficult to tell whether Hamlet is mad or whether he is feigning madness. **In the famous bedroom scene, Hamlet's behaviour towards Gertrude and his murder of Polonius seem to convince us that he is not completely stable, and yet he does try to get through to his mother by showing her how she has erred. In addition, when the ghost enters....**

In the revised passage, the plot summary has been eliminated, or rather, it has been reworked into a sentence that is argumentative. This is what you should strive for when you are writing about a work of literature. When you need to refer to a specific event in the story, you do not have to take a time-out to start recounting the events of the plot, but instead can suggest what is happening while sticking to your argument.

Practical Tip:

One of the reasons why university writing students are prone to having a great deal of plot summary in their literary essays is that they may have been taught in high school to assume that the reader is not familiar with the subject of their essay and needs to be guided along. However, a university-level paper should assume that the reader is *very familiar* with the work of literature being discussed and does not need to be told the events of the story.

23. Misused Single 'Quotation' Marks

The Problem: | Whenever 'government' leaders discuss the economy during a recession, they always seem to find fault with a previous 'administration.'

Errors involving the use of single quotation marks are typically found in at least one quarter of the essays that I read during a semester. Here the writer is using single-quotation marks to give a kind of ironic slant to the terms they enclose, but not only is this ineffective—there does not seem to be any reason why the writer chose to put an ironic emphasis on "government" and "administration"—it is also incorrect: double, and not single, quotation marks are used to indicate that you are undercutting the traditional meaning of a particular word or phrase.

The Solution: | Whenever government leaders discuss the economy during a recession, they always seem to find fault with a previous administration.

Omitting any quotation marks in this sentence is probably best; perhaps double quotation marks could be put around the term "leaders" in an effort to challenge the idea that government representatives are really proficient in leading their constituents. There is only one instance in which you should use single quotation marks, and that is when you are presenting the reader with a quotation that occurs within a pre-existing quotation. An example is found in the following sentence:

As Martin Gardner argues, "'Catching a crab' is rowing slang for a faulty stroke in which the oar is dipped so deeply in the water that the boat's motion, if rapid enough, can send the oar handle against the rower's chest with enough force to unseat him" (241).

The single quotation marks are appropriate because they are being used to indicate a quote from a work of literature that a particular critic has chosen to discuss in his book.

Practical Exercise:

Correct any quotation mark errors in the sentences below:

1. The supervisor 'told' him that 'he had better not say he was "finished" unless he was.'

2. The patient said he was 'under the weather' but the nurse didn't "buy" it for a minute.

3. 'How long will it be before she says "hello" to us,' I wonder.

22. The Plastic Essay

The Problem:

> "Here, professor, I have my essay for you. I've put it in this nice plastic cover in an effort to make it look ever-so-special!"

There is always at least one student in every class who submits the first couple of essays during the term in some sort of plastic contraption. I am very familiar with this practice both as an instructor and as a former student. Admittedly, I was a multiple repeat offender in this category, thinking that my precious plastic cover and accompanying multicoloured spine would prove the difference between A and A+. If only I had taken as much care with the content of my essays as I did with selecting the "perfect" cover.

The problem with using a plastic cover is that it contributes absolutely nothing to the presentation of a paper and in fact serves only to annoy the professor. Usually, the plastic cover has to be removed in order to mark the paper because there is no room to put comments in the left margin and it is difficult, indeed sometimes impossible, to keep the essay open to a particular page without using both hands. If you think for a moment about your professor's growing sense of frustration as he or she finds it impossible to sip that precious cup of coffee while marking your paper because the other hand is having to hold down your uncooperative paper…well, then you'll probably avoid any thought of submitting a "plastic essay" in the future.

The Solution:

> "Here, professor, I have my essay for you. I've used a single staple (or paper clip) and affixed it to the top left-hand corner of the paper."

Using a single staple or paper clip is the most professional manner in which to submit a paper. If you are taking a course in Business and Technical Writing and are submitting a formal report, you might consider having it professionally bound, but by no means would you put it inside one of those cheap plastic covers.

Practical Tip:

The use of a plastic cover, marbled expensive paper, and other such non-essential extras can backfire in another way. If your essay, for instance, has a large number of typographical errors, or has incorrect pagination, or a poor title, or a disorganized bibliography, the effect of these errors on the professor may be more acute because in the back of his or her mind is the thought that the student has only taken this much care in the physical appearance of the essay in an effort to conceal its deficiencies. Believe me, the thought does cross our minds!

21. Redundancy Redundancy

The Problem:

> It would have been both naive **and innocent** of the FBI not to recognize that the smugglers had the means, motive, opportunity, **and wherewithal** to carry out **the day-to-day** operations of their **nefarious** criminal enterprise.

The occasional redundancy is understandable—in an effort to be as detailed as possible about a particular portion of our argument we might fall into the temptation of using a couple of words or phrases that mean much the same thing. However, a chronic problem with redundancy often indicates to the professor that the student is struggling to come up with things to say in the essay. Since this is never the impression we want to make in our writing, it is important to eliminate redundancy whenever possible.

The Solution:

> It would have been naive of the FBI not to recognize that the smugglers had the means, motive, and opportunity to carry out their criminal enterprise.

I am not sure I like saying "means, motive, and opportunity" because it sounds a bit cliché, but this revised sentence is a vast improvement on the one given above. The terms "naive" and "innocent" are too close in meaning for there to be any appreciable difference between them in the context in which they are being used. Similarly, we don't need to indicate that the smugglers have the "wherewithal" to run a criminal enterprise since we know that they have the "means" (this term is broad enough to include the idea that the smugglers are of sufficient intellectual competence to be smuggling). The word "nefarious" means evil or wicked, but does this need to be stressed when we are talking about the criminal act of smuggling? In addition, "day-to-day operations" strikes us as filler and can be removed without changing our understanding of the sentence.

Practical Exercise:

For each of the sentences given below, eliminate any redundancy.

1. Young people can often get caught up in hate groups that profess a narrow-minded, intolerant brand of bigotry.

2. The eroding rock formation was deteriorating rapidly as the constant pounding of the waves wore it down.

3. The Canucks had equalized the score by tying the game and then took the lead by scoring the go-ahead goal with time winding down in the third and final period.

20. The Passionate Appeal Gone Horribly Awry

The Problem: A country that condones capital punishment is a country of vicious, cold-blooded savages who are no better than the criminals they condemn.

"The Passionate Appeal Gone Horribly Awry" usually rears its head in an essay on a very controversial subject, like abortion, euthanasia, or, in this case, capital punishment. What happens in these sorts of appeals is that writers get the idea that by viciously condemning their opponents they will reveal themselves to be in an unassailable position of right and proper moral virtue. However, if there is such a position to be achieved in coming to terms with these very controversial issues, why are they still controversial? When we are writing about a highly charged social issue we need to temper our appeal to *pathos* (emotion) with appeals to *logos* (reason) and *ethos* (moral character). Otherwise, we risk having the reader reject our paper on the basis that we have been carried away by our own emotional attachment to the subject matter.

The Solution: A country that condones capital punishment is a country that demonstrates a fundamental inability to find solutions to violence except through violence.

In our corrected sentence, we have managed to tone down the explicit anger of our original statement. Now, we will not risk alienating the reader who still thinks that capital punishment is justified in the case of serious crimes. We are still making an accusation about what the use of capital punishment says about the society that practises it, but we are no longer making a personal attack on the reader by calling him or her a "vicious, cold-blooded savage" (hardly a fair accusation anyway).

Practical Exercise:

For each of the following sentences, temper its appeal to emotion with appeals to reason and moral character.

1. Is there anything worse than seeing a baby seal drenched in its mother's blood?

2. Those "liberals" who want to reform violent offenders are not living in the real world.

3. You may think euthanasia is a good idea until someone wants to pull the plug on you.

4. The miserable butchers who clear-cut our forests are uncaring and irresponsible.

19. The Fused or Run-On Sentence

The Problem:

> Video games are not as addictive as everyone says they are educational and teach kids important skills.

We have already met the comma splice which, you will remember, is when we take two independent statements and join them with a comma. This we cannot do because either a period, a semi-colon, or a comma with a coordinating conjunction needs to come between two independent statements. In a run-on or fused sentence, two independent statements are thrown together without any attempt to punctuate at all. This frequently happens in an in-class essay, especially when a student changes thought in mid-sentence, as appears to be the case in the above example. The writer had the idea that "Video games are not as addictive as everyone says they are," and also the idea that "they are educational and teach kids important skills." When the writer got to the middle of the sentence he took his second idea and began overwriting his first, with the result being a fused or run-on sentence.

The Solution:

> Video games are not as addictive as everyone says they are. **In fact, these games are educational and teach kids important skills.**

Putting a comma after "says" in the original sentence would not have helped us because this would have formed a comma splice. In addition, although putting a comma after "addictive" almost seems to correct the original run-on sentence, now it makes no sense ("Video games are not as addictive [presumably, as something that the writer was talking about in the previous sentence] *because* everyone says they are educational and teach kids important skills"—this, of course, is a *non sequitur!* Something can be addictive regardless of whether people say it is educational or teaches important skills).

73

Practical Exercise:

Correct the following run-on sentences by using either a period, a semi-colon, or a comma with a coordinating conjunction.

1. Individuals would be carried up to the altar there they would be sacrificed.

2. Archaeologists recently found the remains of an ancient human are causing quite a stir.

3. The Quebec-based *Unibroue* is famous for "Maudite" this beer is simply outstanding.

4. The latest *Star Wars* film set box office records it did not do so well with reviewers.

18. The Four Horsemen of the Logic Apocalypse

The Problem:

> You cannot trust his opinion about the potential dangers of our crib mattress—**he does not even have a university education. Besides, 50,000 satisfied customers and a 90% approval rating for the product are what really tell the story.** I suppose with these kinds of community watch-dog nay-sayers, **you can lead them to the water but you can't make them drink.**

The Argument to the Person, the Bandwagon Argument, the False Analogy, and Card Stacking and Special Pleading are what I call "The Four Horsemen of the Logic Apocalypse." These logical errors occasionally make an appearance in our writing, and while they seem to work in television advertising and in the courtroom, they should be avoided at all costs in a formal essay. Our problem passage begins with an argument *ad hominem,* an attack against a person rather than an argument: the crib-mattress critic is ridiculed for not having a university education. However, what does having a university education have to do with knowing whether or not a crib mattress is safe? The writer has made a logical error in avoiding the criticism by attacking the person who made it. The writer then follows this Argument to the Person with a Bandwagon argument (or argument *ad populem*): "50,000 satisfied customers and a 90% approval rating for the product are what really tell the story." However, the opinion of the majority is not always right, even in a democracy. The majority opinion often gets the majority what it wants, but what it ends up getting for itself is not always "good" or "right" or even what is best for it. In addition, the writer is using the product's 90% approval rating as a good thing, but ignoring crucial evidence on the other side of the argument (this is a form of Card Stacking or Special Pleading): that 10% of their clients did not approve of the product (this works out to more than 5,500 customers!). Finally, the writer

concludes by making a false analogy, a comparison in which the differences between the things being compared outweigh the similarities. Comparing critics
of a crib-mattress to animals that can be led to water but not made to drink simply makes no sense.

The Solution:

> Although there have been criticisms made of our product,
> we have had many satisfied customers, and those who have
> returned the crib mattress have received a full refund.

What a difference removing logical errors makes to a passage of prose! By
admitting that the crib-mattress is not foolproof, the writer avoids looking as
though he or she is desperate to conceal the product's shortcomings by unnec-
essarily attacking its opponents.

Practical Exercise:

Examine the following sentences and identify any logical errors that you
find. How could the sentences be reworked to eliminate these errors?

1. The Cabinet Member would never make a good Prime Minister because
   you can't teach an old dog new tricks.

2. Ladies and gentlemen of the jury, how can we trust that the witness really
   saw my client shoot the victim if he has been convicted of marijuana
   possession?

3. I could believe what she has to say about the issue if she wasn't such a
   jerk.

4. He wants to introduce a new budget to better manage the finances of our
   nation, but at the same time he's running around having an affair with his
   intern!

5. If the gloves don't fit, you must acquit.

6. You must be the only person I know who has not yet bought a Pentium
   computer.

7. Although my client has been convicted of second-degree murder, sending
   him to jail for life would be like executing a child for stealing a piece of
   candy.

17. The Mis;placed Semi-colon

The Problem:

> Research has shown that about 50% of marriages end in divorce; but this figure is arguably inflated, however, it still shows that we have some work to do to improve domestic relationships.

Misplacement and misuse of the semi-colon occur in about three quarters of the papers I read during the course of a term. One of the reasons that this error occurs so frequently is that as writers develop their abilities to write longer and more complex sentences, they run into difficulties punctuating them. They have been encouraged by previous teachers to write complex and compound sentences, but they have not always managed to get a handle on when commas and semi-colons should and should not be used. In the above sentence, the student would have had a grammatically correct statement if she had switched the two underlined punctuation marks, putting the comma before the co-ordinating conjunction "but" and putting the semi-colon before the conjunctive adverb "however."

The Solution:

> Research has shown that about 50% of marriages end in divorce, but this figure is arguably inflated; however, it still shows that we have some work to do to improve domestic relationships.

In our corrected sentence, the semi-colon separates two statements that can stand alone as sentences, and indeed, there are really only two instances in which you should use semi-colons: (1) between independent clauses whose content is related, and (2) between items in a list which contain commas. An example of the second case, which admittedly does not occur very often, is the following:

Fifty Fatal Flaws

> The winners of the lottery came from London, Ontario;
> Antigonish, Nova Scotia; and Nanaimo, British
> Columbia.

You can see in the above example that if commas were used to separate each of these three places, someone unfamiliar with Canada might make the mistake of thinking that the winners came from six different locations!

Practical Tip:

Whenever you find yourself writing a fairly complex sentence and getting the urge to punctuate it with a semi-colon, check to make sure that what comes before the semi-colon and what comes after it can both stand by themselves as sentences. Remember that this always has to be the case unless you are separating items in a list.

16. The G I A N T Block Quote

The Problem:

> As Johann Huizinga argues in *Homo Ludens: A Study of the Play Element in Culture*:
>
> > There can be no doubt that this ideal of chivalry, loyalty, courage and self-control has contributed much to the civilization that upheld it. Even if the greater part of it was fiction and fantasy, in public life and in education it certainly raised the tone. But under the influence of epic and romantic fancy the historical image of such peoples as professed that ideal often underwent an enchanted transformation, which sometimes induced even the gentlest spirits to praise war, seen through this mirage of chivalrous tradition, more loudly than the reality has ever deserved. (102-103)
>
> Huizinga then goes on to suggest that....

When you are writing an essay that is less than five pages, it is not rhetorically effective to incorporate large block quotations into your essay, especially a series of such quotations. With so little space in which to put forth your argument, you cannot afford to have this space occupied with someone else's critical opinion. In addition, if you have a series of block quotations from a single source, you risk having your essay look like the Single Source Research Paper discussed earlier.

The Solution:

> In *Homo Ludens: A Study of the Play Element in Culture*, Johann Huizinga argues that the "ideal of chivalry, loyalty, courage and self-control has contributed much to the civilization that upheld it" (102-103). This is an important idea because it suggests that....

In the revised passage, the writer has condensed the quotation and is immediately prepared to discuss it (in the original passage, she was about to launch into additional critical commentary). It is so important in an essay to make your argument first, then introduce a quote or paraphrase that supports it, and then discuss the critical quotation to explain how you situate your own position in relation to it.

Practical Tip:

Remember that in a thousand-word essay, having two or three large block quotations of one hundred and fifty words or so can take up nearly half of your available word limit.

15. The Two-Sentence Conclusion

The Problem:

> Hollywood films have got to eliminate their disturbing preoccupation with sex and violence if they want to win back older audiences. If they are prepared to do this, we may see a return to the golden age of the Silver Screen.

There is nothing more disappointing for a reader than to get to the conclusion of an essay and find that it is only a sentence or two in length. Although the conclusion should not introduce any new material, it should be a place where you restate your thesis in different terms, discuss the importance of your findings, and perhaps show how your essay opens the way for further research in the subject you have been exploring. In the example above, there seems to be only a restatement of a portion of the thesis statement, and this is followed by a remark that seems designed to extricate the writer from the essay.

The Solution:

> Hollywood films are alienating older audiences because they have a disturbing preoccupation with sex and violence and an inability, it seems, to divorce the two. Studies have shown that attendance at R-rated films by seniors has steadily declined over the past decade, and thus these films have alienated an important client base. Although increased attendance at R-rated films by young adults has helped to bridge this gap, seniors have been left either to attend the latest Disney film with their grandchildren or rent a video. Perhaps by exploiting the nostalgia of this disgruntled fan base, Hollywood film-makers can bring back a return to the golden age of the Silver Screen.

As we can see in our revised paragraph, the writer has done well to create a much more memorable conclusion than what we saw previously. The initial sentence restates the thesis of the paper, and this is followed by a sentence that explains the significance of Hollywood's preoccupation with sex and violence: a decrease in attendance at R-rated films by seniors. The third sentence develops upon this by explaining the position seniors have been left in by the direction Hollywood film-making has taken, and the conclusion ends with a suggestion about how seniors can be won back to the movies.

Practical Tip:

Under no circumstances should you either apologize for something in your essay in the conclusion, or make an offhand comment that undercuts what you have been saying.

14. Poor Organization

The Problem:

> Alfred Lord Tennyson is often considered an orthodox Victorian writer and Lewis Carroll is considered an Anti-Victorian writer. Tennyson is seen as a Victorian because in much of his poetry he upholds Victorian ideals while Carroll is perceived as Anti-Victorian because he is so often critical of Victorian ideals. Tennyson was poet laureate and so wrote a number of poems to commemorate state events, but Carroll remained a writer of children's books and mathematical texts all his life.

The above passage suffers from poor organization on two levels. In one sense, the paragraph has a great deal of repetition, in part because of the awkward manner in which the student is flipping back and forth in his discussion of the two writers. Thus, the term "Victorian" makes six appearances in the first two sentences. However, there is also poor organization in the sense that the writer is not allowing himself any space to develop his interesting ideas. He has a bunch of information that he is lumping into one paragraph and he is rapidly switching back and forth to make sure that he is covering all of his points. In order to make a meaningful argument, the writer needs to develop each of these fine points; otherwise, the essay begins to sound like a history lesson rather than a well-organized, critical investigation of two literary figures.

The Solution:

> One of the ways that we can see Alfred Lord Tennyson as an orthodox Victorian writer and Lewis Carroll as an Anti-Victorian writer is by examining their major works....
>
> We also see the fundamental differences in Tennyson's and Carroll's attitudes towards the Victorian age in which they lived by examining the influence of their public lives on their private writings....

Instead of putting a whole bunch of undeveloped information together, the revised passage shows how the writer has separated out his key ideas and organized them into distinct paragraphs. In an effort to show the differences between Tennyson and Carroll, the writer will first compare their major works and then move on to examine the influence of their public lives on their private writings. The reader now knows precisely what to expect, with these clearly defined topic sentences preparing him or her for the arguments to follow.

13. The Wrong Preposition

The Problem: | **In** the end of the novel, Helen Huntingdon and Gilbert Markham are married.

Probably forty percent of student essays that I read have at least one preposition error, and of these a small number have systemic preposition problems which prevent the essays from passing. Teaching someone what preposition to use in a particular circumstance is difficult, because once you cover a number of basic cases, there are no clearly defined rules for which specific words or phrases take which prepositions. In addition, most words and phrases take a number of different prepositions which dramatically change their meaning in a particular context (e.g., being afraid "of" someone is completely different from being afraid "for" someone). Students with systemic preposition problems should get hold of a good grammar handbook in order to familiarize themselves with the basic instances in which each preposition is used.

The Solution: | **At** the end of the novel, Helen Huntingdon and Gilbert Markham are married.

The original preposition error in the problem sentence was likely made because the prepositional phrase "In the end..." does exist and is, in fact, quite common. However, when we are talking about location in a novel, it is correct to say "At the end..." but not "In the end..." (although one would say "In the last few pages" rather than "At the last few pages"). Improving your skill with choosing correct prepositions is one of those things with which reading a bit every day will help enormously.

Practical Exercise:

Determine whether each of the following sentences contains any incorrect or improperly placed prepositions and make the necessary emendations:

1. At what address do you wish to receive your mail at?

2. Make sure that you check for rocks underneath the water before you dive in it.

3. It is important that we remember to divide up the money between the three of us.

4. My parents were very upset about me for staying out so late.

5. The manager disapproved about his assistant working so much overtime.

6. I understood about what you said, but I am still not sure I agree.

12. Slanted Language

The Problem:

> My fellow countrymen, it is my solemn duty to inform you that earlier tonight, our military was forced to make a pre-emptive strike against those powers that threaten our nation. Delivering a series of clean bombs, we successfully hit the enemy target, causing only a minor amount of collateral damage. In this hour of conflict....

Slanted language is language that endeavours to condition a positive response. For instance, when a military force attacks a foreign power, the government does not want to have to tell its citizens that it invaded a foreign country, blew up an ammunition dump where 750 soldiers were stationed, and that the resulting series of explosions destroyed a nearby village, killing another 500 people and wounding several hundreds more. So instead, the Prime Minister or the President (or whoever is in charge) makes a television appearance and regretfully informs the public of the incident by saying something that sounds very much like the passage in the box above. This is slanted language because the Prime Minister or President is trying to make the public not feel so bad about the fact that its nation has just killed several hundred people.

The Solution:

> Earlier tonight, our military attacked a foreign power. Dropping a series of warheads we successfully hit an ammunition depot, killing a total of more than one thousand people both at the ammunition dump and in a nearby village.

The revised sentence gets rid of slanted terms like "delivering," "pre-emptive strike," "clean bombs," and "collateral damage" which conceal the truth about what they really are. Whenever you are writing an essay, you have to be wary of using slanted language in an effort to convince the reader of your case. Similarly, whenever you are reading secondary sources, you must be careful not to incorporate information into your essay that contains slanted language unless you are prepared to expose it for what it is.

Practical Exercise:

Connected with slanted language is propaganda, which is an organized campaign of slanted language that is used either to promote or to attack a particular organization or movement. When we think of propaganda, we typically think of the Nazi campaign against the Jews during World War II, but propaganda is on our television screens day in and day out in commercials. As an exercise, you might examine a series of commericals in order to learn the slogans of different companies and then examine whether or not these slogans are effective propaganda.

11. The "It is because…" Construction

The Problem:

> It is **because** of its lightning-quick ability to spring upon its prey that the California Trapdoor Spider is a successful predator.

On the surface, there does not seem to be anything that awful with using the expression "It is because," but there is almost always an improvement that can be made in a sentence that contains this phrase. The "it" in this sentence is sometimes called the *indefinite "it"* but I like to call it the *nothing "it"* because if you try to figure out what it is referring to you will probably come up with "nothing." There are a whole host of phrases that begin with the *nothing "it,"* like "it is for this reason that," "it is interesting that," and "it is conceivable that." Whenever these phrases appear in your formal essay writing they should be expunged because usually they are tacked onto (and therefore simply weaken) an excellent pre-existing sentence.

The Solution:

> The California Trapdoor Spider is a successful predator **because of its lightning-quick ability to spring upon its prey.**

You will notice that our revised sentence contains exactly three less words than the original, having lost the "It is" and a "that." Turning the sentence around is important too because it puts the spider, which is really what we are talking about, at the beginning. The original sentence delays things by telling us what the spider does before it introduces us to the spider itself. When you are proofreading the final draft of your paper, do a word search of the phrases "is because" and "was because" to see if you have any of these constructions in your essay.

Practical Exercise:

Revise the following sentences and remove any words or phrases that are superfluous.

1. It is clearly the opinion of this writer that it was because of the D-Day invasion that the tide of World War II was changed.

2. The reason marathon runners are able to run such great distances is because they are able to overcome their body's build-up of lactic acid through superior conditioning.

3. It is interesting to note that it was only two months ago that the school year ended.

4. It is amazing and also encouraging to see such an improvement in the patient.

10. Padding

The Problem:

> Smoking causes numerous **debilitating** health problems **which can seriously compromise one's safety and well-being.** These health problems include **the terrors of** bronchitis **and bronchial inflamation**, emphysema (**quite simply, a ravaging condition with devastating effects**), **fatal** lung cancer (**as well as throat and mouth cancer**), **a disturbing** yellowing of the skin, and **irreparably** damaged cilia in the throat and nasal passages.

The above passage is a perfect example of "Padding." The student needs to write a 750-word essay on the dangers of smoking (let's say, in public restaurants) but really only has about 350-400 words of solid argument. He chose this topic thinking it would be easy, but now realizes that he has very little to say about it and therefore must resort to saying things in the most roundabout way in order to meet the assigned word count. This tactic, however, is going to play havoc with his grade.

The Solution:

> Smoking causes numerous health problems, including bronchitis, emphysema, lung cancer, yellowing of the skin, and damaged cilia in the throat and nasal passages.

In our revised passage we have dropped thirty-seven of the sixty words in our original sentence and eliminated all of the padding. As you can see, *padding* is like *redundancy*, but when it occurs throughout an entire paper it can be a much more serious problem.

Practical Exercise:

For each of the following sentences, remove any unnecessary padding.

1. Being completely and utterly unable to speak the foreign language of the country I found myself in, I pathetically resorted to using an amusing mixture of hand signals.

2. Openly admitting his mistake was an exceedingly important first step on his long and difficult road to discovering his own inner being.

3. The fierce cheetah can quickly generate land speeds in excess of 65 mph.

4. Doing up the latch of your seat belt and correctly positioning the cross strap against your body is a crucial procedure in the timely prevention of devastating automobile accidents that happen day in and day out on our city streets.

9. The Run-Away Thesaurus

The Problem:

> The President demonstrated a **profound lack of abstemiousness** by **surreptitiously engaging** in an illicit relationship with a **gregarious** White House intern.

Yikes, put away that thesaurus…you're killing me! Indeed, a thesaurus in the wrong student's hands can be a very dangerous weapon, as he or she begins to launch multisyllabic missiles at the reader. The most significant problem with using a thesaurus is that it breaks the number one rule of good essay writing: use simple words to express complex ideas rather than the other way around. However, another problem with constantly consulting a thesaurus is that it is apt to give us a word that means *almost* the same thing as the word we want to replace, *but not quite*. Also, when we use a thesaurus once, we have a tendency to want to use it again and again, so that every sentence in our essay can sound as "professional" as the one we just fixed up.

The Solution:

> The President showed a lack of judgment by having an affair with a White House intern.

With the thesaurus safely tucked away, we now have a sentence that actually gets to the point and makes some sense. As we can see, abusing the thesaurus can work hand in hand with a desire to add *padding* to our essay, as we replace our simply-worded complex ideas with complexly worded simple ideas.

Practical Exercise:

Someone has taken out a thesaurus and refused to write a clear sentence. Examine the following sentences and bring them back down to earth.

1. The policeman's malfeasance permitted the malefactor to evade just punishment.

2. The firefighting *deus ex machina* snatched the stranded feline out of the arbor vitae.

3. Might I enquire as to your particular appellation?

4. The ectomorphic high jumper had little problem eclipsing the bar.

5. That *enfant terrible* does nothing but enervate me.

6. Although a puissant king, he behaved in a puerile fashion.

7. It is difficult to be punctilious when everyone else is so rumbustious and rude.

8. The Uninspired Topic Sentence

The Problem:

> Anne Brontë's second novel, *The Tenant of Wildfell Hall,* was published in 1848. Its depiction of a central female character who is treated miserably by her husband and who takes action to extricate herself from this destructive relationship caused its first male readers a profound degree of discomfort. Brontë sets her story in the Regency Period but is nonetheless condemning certain patriarchal attitudes that carried over into the Victorian era....

A topic sentence is a sentence at the beginning of a body paragraph which refers back to a specific part of the thesis and clearly tells the reader what you will be discussing in this section of the essay. Just as the first sentence of the conclusion should restate the thesis in different terms, the first sentence of a body paragraph *should restate a portion of the thesis in different terms.* In the above example, the writer has chosen to begin her paragraph by introducing factual information that is utterly irrelevant to what follows. When you read a topic sentence, you should be perfectly clear about what the following sentences will discuss, but the above topic sentence does not give any indication of what will be discussed, except that it will probably have something to do with *The Tenant of Wildfell Hall.*

The Solution:

> In Anne Brontë's *The Tenant of Wildfell Hall,* the depiction of a central female character who is treated miserably by her husband and who takes action to extricate herself from this destructive relationship caused its first male readers a profound degree of discomfort. Brontë sets her story in the Regency Period but is nonetheless condemning certain patriarchal attitudes that carried over into the Victorian era....

If the writer wants to discuss the effect that *The Tenant of Wildfell Hall* had on early male readership then the revised topic sentence (basically, our second sentence from the original passage) is much more appropriate than merely giving the publication date of the novel. When the reader comes to this revised topic sentence, he or she immediately understands the kind of argument that the writer is laying out. You should think of topic sentences in the same way that you think about your thesis statement—you cannot possibly write a persuasive essay without some kind of thesis statement because the reader would have no idea what to expect. Similarly, a well-developed topic sentence must begin each of the body paragraphs so that readers recognize where they are and know where they are going.

7. (A)rticle Errors

The Problem: | Internet is **a** invaluable resource that is often unfairly criticized.

A number of article errors in an essay will always prevent it from passing. Like using the wrong preposition, getting the articles "a," "an," and "the" wrong is a rudimentary grammatical error that a professor is duty-bound to punish severely. The words "a" and "an" are indefinite articles that are used to designate nouns which are members of a class or group. Thus, "a hammer" is any one of the group of instruments that share all of the characteristics that define what a hammer is, and "an elephant" is any one of the group of animals that share all of the characteristics that define what an elephant is. The definite article, "the," is used to refer to a very specific person, place, or thing that may or may not be contained within a larger group. So "the hammer" is a very particular hammer, like "the hammer on the table over there," and "the elephant" is a very specific elephant, like "the elephant I saw yesterday at the zoo."

The Solution: | **The** Internet is **an** invaluable resource that is often unfairly criticized.

You might be wondering why we usually talk about "the Internet" and seldom about "an Internet," but we can explain this now rather easily by taking into consideration our arguments above. The "Internet" is a specific individual item that is not the member of any group: or rather, it is the member of a group that contains only itself as a member. There are not millions, or even thousands, or even two Internets floating around—there is just the one (there might be millions of computers, thousands of Internet service providers, and hundreds of search engines, but there is only one Internet). Therefore, because "a" and "an" are indefinite articles that refer in an unspecific way to members of a particular class or group, and because the "Internet" is always specific—being the only member of its group—it takes the definite article "the."

Practical Exercise:

For each of the sentences below, determine if there are article errors and correct them.

1. Day before yesterday, we visited a historic landmark on Thames River.

2. Where is subway station? I saw it yesterday when we were looking for an hotel.

3. Time for rest is over. Now we must take active part in saving the forests.

4. Office hours for the professor will be cancelled for a week or two.

6. Agreement Errors

The Problem: The group of composition students **are** writing the final examination.

A chronic problem with agreement errors will almost always prevent a paper from receiving a passing grade, so it is important to learn the various situations in which agreement errors most commonly occur and then be careful to watch for these when you are proofreading your essay. The example above is one of those tricky situations in which even an experienced writer can fall victim to an agreement error. The difficulty lies in the fact that the word which comes right before the verb is plural, but is not the subject of the sentence. The verb seems like it should agree with "students," but "group" is in fact the subject. The word "students" is part of a prepositional phrase that describes "group" but does not make that group plural, because then "group" would be "groups."

The Solution: The group of composition students **is** writing the final examination.

Often writers who would not normally make agreement errors on a take-home paper will make them during an in-class essay, because in a particular sentence they will be tricked by a noun that is in closer proximity to the verb than the subject. When this situation arises, you always need to check whether that noun beside the verb is the subject, or is only part of a prepositional phrase that describes the subject.

Practical Exercise:

For each of the following sentences, determine whether or not there is an agreement error and then make corrections if necessary:

1. A herd of pigs are often difficult to control if they are not regularly fed.

2. Either the chairman or his assistant is going to see that the issue is resolved.

3. Shakespeare's understanding of dramatic action and his construction of plot are what makes his later tragedies so incredibly powerful.

4. A hiker's worst nightmare are changing weather conditions.

5. Before the exam come hours and hours of studying.

6. Each of the players are ready for the upcoming game, but only one of them are going to start.

5. Th Typographical Error

The Problem: | Typograpical errors ar incredibly fustrating for readrs. |

If you asked me what I thought the single worst error to make in a paper was, I would tell you without any hesitation that it is the *typographical error.* Typographical errors—missing letters, extra spaces, periods where there are supposed to be commas, first words of sentences not capitalized—are not the result of ignorance but of neglect. Typographical errors come about when an essay has not been proofread, when the writer has not printed out the essay before proofreading, or when it has been written at the last minute. The reason it is so dangerous to have typos in an essay is that the professor is justified in giving the paper almost any mark (except perhaps an A, which is presumably what we are aiming for). Some professors become absolutely incensed by multiple typographical errors in the same essay, and they almost always go on about it in their final comments (which is bad, right, because they write them just before or just after they give you a grade).

The Solution: | Typographical errors are incredibly frustrating for readers. |

The only ways to correct a problem with typographical errors are to avoid beginning a paper the night before it is due and to make sure that you proofread your work a number of times, both while you are writing it and after you think it is typographically "perfect."

Practical Exercise:

In the passage below there are twenty typographical errors. Give yourself ten minutes or so and see if you can find them all.

Haveyou ever seen a child playing with a set of buildng building blocks, Th child takess he blocks and begin to stack the m until they form a shape that pleases the the tot. Once the child becames bored with the shape—oh. after a

101

minute or so—he or she knocks knocks the blocks over and begins building a different structure.Cubist painters did very much the same thng with the subjects they used for their paintings. Cubism reduces things to toelemental shapes, like lines and gemetric planes. and then attempts to recontruct images from them.

4. Undermining the Thesis

The Problem:

> Although the Internet should be more vigorously monitored for criminal activities, opponents of this idea raise some good points. They suggest that our personal freedoms would be sacrificed, and that protecting a small minority of users while denying others their right to acquire certain types of information would be unconstitutional. I kind of agree with this idea...

Many instructors encourage their students to introduce opposing points of view into their essay because refusing to acknowledge the arguments of your opponents weakens your own. However, professors do not want their students to introduce these opposing points of view *and then go on to agree with them.* We introduce an opponent's argument to show the flaws in its reasoning, and thus by extension, to validate our own conclusions. In the above example, the writer is discussing the importance of monitoring the Internet, but in the course of doing so, she begins to agree with her opponent's argument. Consequently, she undermines her own thesis and compromises the integrity of her paper.

The Solution:

> Although the Internet should be more vigorously monitored for criminal activities, opponents of this idea raise a number of objections. They suggest that our personal freedoms would be sacrificed, and that protecting a small minority of users while denying others their right to acquire certain types of information would be unconstitutional. **However, it is precisely this kind of self-serving rhetoric that puts our children in danger. Opponents of Internet monitoring are trying to hide behind an archaic constitution that was written before we had the technological capacity to design something as complicated as the Internet, and furthermore...**

You can see that in our revised paragraph, our opponent's argument is introduced only in an effort to expose its flaws and tear it apart. This makes for very effective prose.

Practical Exercise:

Take an issue that you feel strongly about, come up with a thesis statement, and write an introduction that begins by summarizing your opponent's argument in a sentence or two. However, immediately expose the flaws in this argument by introducing your own counter argument and then quickly bring the reader to your thesis statement.

3. Sentence Fragments

The Problem:

> To be able to leap out of a plane at 10,000 feet and plummet toward the earth, feeling the air rush past you at incredible speeds.

Sentence fragments are major grammatical errors that can mean the difference not simply between receiving a B or a B+ on your paper, but receiving an A or an F. Fragments are more common on in-class essays and final exams than on take-home papers, mostly because we tend to make them when our minds are skipping back and forth between ideas. The sentence fragment above is a classic example: the sentence begins with an infinitive but it does not contain a conjugated verb. Writers sometimes get confused when beginning a sentence in this way because they fail to see that the infinitive, an *unconjugated verb*, is a *subject* that needs to take a *conjugated verb*.

Other common sentence fragments are formed when writers begin simple sentences with conjunctions like "and," "but," "for," etc. It is perfectly fine to begin a sentence with one of these words provided that it *is introducing a dependent clause* which in turn *is introducing an independent clause*. For instance, you would never write the sentence fragment, "For I am not old enough to go." However, you could write the complete sentence, "For although I am not old enough to go, you are not old enough to go either."

The Solution:

> **It must be amazing** to be able to leap out of a plane at 10,000 feet and plummet toward the earth, feeling the air rush past you at incredible speeds.

Our sentence now has a subject *and* a verb. I am still not completely crazy about its construction (perhaps I could mess with it some more), but at least it's now *a sentence*.

Practical Exercise:

Always double check sentences in your essay that begin with the word "To," because if they are forming infinitive subjects, you need to check that they have a conjugated verb along with them. Try your hand at correcting the following fragments.

1. Even if she did come back after curfew.

2. And then the honourable member was forced to concede this point.

3. To be able to say that convincingly, without even batting an eyelash.

4. It is an amazing feeling. To create something with your bare hands.

2. Incomplete Thesis Statement

The Problem: | Santa Claus is a dangerous role model for children. |

Your high-school English teacher probably lectured you about the importance of having a thesis statement in your essay. He or she would have said something like this: "As the final sentence of your introductory paragraph, a thesis statement serves to state the argument of your paper and to indicate that the matter you are treating is presented in a logical and coherent manner." I want you to forget that definition for a minute and think about this one: "A thesis statement is *a map of the place where you want to take your readers.*" Readers want to know that the place they are going to is interesting, and if you refuse to tell them, the chances are that they are not going to stick around for the trip.

The Solution: | Santa Claus is a dangerous role model for children because he is racist, sexist, and elitist. |

You may have been told that a thesis statement is the argument that you are going to make to the reader, but you may have not been told that it is a bit more complicated than that. Someone who reads one of your essays wants to know not only where you are going, but also how you are going to get there. If I told you that Santa Claus was a negative influence on children, you might not believe me, but if I told you that Santa Claus was a dangerous role model for children because his manner of distributing gifts discriminates on the basis of race, sex, and class, you would at least ask me to explain what the heck I was talking about. This is precisely the hook you need to elicit the appropriate kind of psychological response from the reader. Our corrected thesis statement above contains both *what we are going to prove* and *how we are going to prove it*. Without these two parts to our sentence, we simply do not have a thesis statement.

Practical Exercise:

Correct the following incomplete thesis statements by including *how* you would go about proving these various arguments.

1. Capital punishment should be reinstated for those who commit first-degree murder.

2. Marital infidelity should be an impeachable offense for elected officials.

3. Video games are a valuable learning tool for children.

4. The procedure for distributing parking passes at our university needs to be changed.

5. Television is a far more interesting medium than film.

1. Plagiarism

The Problem:

> I would argue that part of the confusion about whether Bakhtin was a phenomenologist, a carnival clown, or a Russian Orthodox Christian stems from the fact that he shared with his Marxist associates an opposition to certain ideological trends then current.

The sentence above is an example of *plagiarism*, a form of academic dishonesty in which a student takes either the words or ideas of another writer without acknowledging where these words or ideas come from. Of the fifty fatal flaws of essay writing, this one is the most fatal. If the student plagiarises an essay, the appropriate Dean is notified and the student receives either a zero in the course with the notation "Academic Dishonesty" permanently marked on his or her transcript or the student is expelled from the university. In either case, there is a permanent record of the student's plagiarism. Students should be aware that professors know about essays purchased either from paper mills or from on-line databases, that they are familiar with these web sites, and that in the past they have had little problem tracking down plagiarised essays regardless of any assurances a prospective web site gives concerning confidentiality.

The Solution:

> As Caryl Emerson argues, "part of the confusion [about Bakhtin's identity] stems from the fact that [he] shared with his Marxist associates an opposition to certain ideological trends then current" (243).

If you take a direct quotation from a source, it must be enclosed in quotation marks and parenthetically referenced. If you paraphrase a source—take the ideas of a source and express them in your own words—you must still use parenthetical documentation to indicate where your paraphrase originates from. If you have any doubts about whether or not you are plagiarising, you must consult your professor to be on the safe side. Another form of academic dishonesty is unfairly slanting or distorting comments made by another scholar. For instance, if a critic claims that a performance of *Hamlet* was so bad that it had people "rising from their seats and heading for the exits," you cannot claim that the critic said the performance was so good that people were "rising from their seats." In other words, you cannot distort or lie about what another critic has said.

Practical Tip:

Always have a definite opinion about a particular topic before you go to the library to use secondary source materials. Also, do not be afraid to have a significant number of critical sources in your bibliography. These can only improve the quality of your essay by placing it within the pre-existing framework of an ongoing debate.

Answers to Selected Questions

48. The Comma Splice

1. The driver does not know how to get there, because he cannot remember the way.

2. Because I could not stop for death, it kindly stopped for me.

3. That student goes to parties, and he never fails to come home drunk.

4. I agree with you, for I happen to think Marx was a genius.

5. Candy is dandy, but liquor is quicker.

47. The Comma Error

1. The sentence is correct.

2. Being upset and disoriented after the accident was the reason the driver fled the scene.

3. The way to open a present is not with caution and reserve, but with reckless abandon.

4. Only when things calmed down and eventually returned to order did he decide that it was eventually time to be going.

5. The sentence is correct.

Fifty Fatal Flaws

44. Spelling Mistakes

1. b	6. b	11. c	16. c	21. b
2. c	7. a	12. c	17. a	22. a
3. c	8. c	13. a	18. a	23. c
4 b	9. a	14. c	19. b	24. a
5. a	10. a	15. c	20. a or c	25. a

42. The Dangling Modifier

1. Returning from his trip overseas, Peter found the house as deserted as he had left it.

2. Acknowledging some mistakes in its recent article, the local newspaper printed a correction.

3. The sentence is correct.

4. Pleased that the weather was gradually improving, the company could introduce the spring fashion line without any fear of poor sales.

38. The Succession of Short Sentences

1. Cyclists often ride dangerously close to cars and should avoid doing so.

2. Because clear-cutting decimates entire sections of forest, we need to do our share in ensuring proper forest management.

3. If you want something fun, relaxing, and easy to do, read a book.

33. Ending (or Not Ending) a Sentence with a Preposition

1. The sentence is correct.

2. I originally came from Hamilton.

3. The sentence is correct.

4. The sentence is correct.

5. Where is the office at which he worked?

6. Computer fantasy role-playing games are addictive.

29. Usage Errors

1. An *allusion* is a reference to someone or something not present; an *illusion* is what David Copperfield does.

2. A *genius* is someone with exceptional ability in a particular area; *ingenious* describes someone or something that is smart or clever.

3. Both *rebut* and *refute* can mean to disprove, although rebut also carries with it the meaning of "forcing or turning back."

4. A word's *denotation* is its literal meaning; a word's *connotations* are its implied meanings.

5. An *amoral* person does not understand the difference between right and wrong (eg., an infant); an *immoral* person understands the difference but chooses to do wrong.

6. A motionless object is *stationary*; writing materials and office sup-plies are *stationery*.

7. *Anxious* and *eager* are both feelings of anticipation, but anxious is a negative feeling and eager is a positive one.

8. To *elicit* is to draw forth; *illicit* means unlawful or forbidden.

9. To *censor* is to suppress objectionable material; to *censure* is to reprimand.

27. The Brutal Bibliography

Allday, Elizabeth. *Stefan Zweig: A Critical Biography.* London: Allen, 1972.

Beckett, Samuel. *Endgame.* New York: Grove, 1978.

Eales, Richard. *Chess: The History of a Game.* London: Batsford, 1985.

Eliot, T. S. *Selected Poems.* London: Faber, 1971.

Fine, Reuben. *The Psychology of the Chess Player.* New York: Dover, 1967.

Fisher, John. *The Magic of Lewis Carroll.* London: Nelson, 1973.

Keyes, Frances Parkinson. *The Chess Players.* New York: Farrar, 1960.

Levy, David and Stewart Reuben. *The Chess Scene.* London: Faber, 1974.

Phillips, Robert, ed. *Aspects of Alice.* New York: Vanguard, 1971.

Waitzkin, Fred, et al. *Searching for Bobby Fischer.* New York: Random, 1988.

26. Using "I believe that," "I think that," and "It is my opinion that"

1. The government can spy on us at will, and this should stop.

2. By banning cellular telephones in cars, we can save lives.

3. The current economic forecast is erroneous.

4. Extraterrestrial life forms exist and are watching us.

23. Misused Single 'Quotation' Marks

1. The supervisor told him that he had better not say he was "finished" unless he was.

2. The patient said he was "under the weather" but the nurse didn't buy it for a minute.

3. "How long will it be before she says 'hello' to us," I wonder.

21. **Redundancy Redundancy**

 1. Young people can often get caught up in hate groups.

 2. The rock formation was deteriorating rapidly from the constant pounding of the waves.

 3. The Canucks tied the game and then took the lead near the end of the third period.

20. **The Passionate Appeal Gone Horribly Awry**

 1. Baby seals are thoughtlessly slaughtered.

 2. The idea of reforming violent offenders works far better in theory than in practice.

 3. Most defenders of euthanasia have never been personally confronted with the issue.

 4. Clearcutting is irresponsible forest management.

19. **The Fused or Run-On Sentence**

 1. Individuals would be carried up to the altar, and there they would be sacrificed.

 2. Archaeologists recently found the remains of an ancient human, and this is causing quite a stir.

 3. The Quebec-based *Unibroue* is famous for "Maudite"; this beer is simply outstanding.

 4. The latest *Star Wars* film set box office records, but did not do so well with reviewers.

18.   **The Four Horsemen of the Logic Apocalypse**

1. The Cabinet Member has demonstrated a certain closemindedness about a number of issues that would prevent him from making an effective Prime Minister.

2. Ladies and gentlemen of the jury, I would advise you to take the witness' potential use of a narcotic into consideration when deciding what he did and did not see.

3. I do not agree with her position on the issue, and the particular manner in which she presents her arguments does not help her win many followers.

4. Our leader has demonstrated an appalling lack of moral judgment.

5. The fact that the prosecution has unsuccessfully attempted to link my client with the murders by forcing him to try on a pair of gloves should be considered during your deliberations.

6. A number of people I know have purchased Pentium computers and are quite happy with them. You should consider doing so yourself.

7. Although my client has been convicted of second-degree murder, sending him to jail for life would be an excessive sentence.

13.   **The Wrong Preposition**

1. At what address do you wish to receive your mail?

2. Make sure that you check for rocks under the water before you dive into it.

3. It is important that we remember to divide up the money among the three of us.

4. My parents were very upset with me for staying out so late.

5. The manager disapproved of his assistant's working so much overtime.

6. I understood what you said, but I am still not sure I agree.

11. The "It is because..." Construction

1. The D-Day invasion changed the tide of World War II.

2. Marathon runners are able to run such great distances because they are able to overcome their body's build-up of lactic acid through superior conditioning.

3. The school year ended only two months ago.

4. The patient's improvement is amazing.

10. Padding

1. I could not speak the language of the country I was in, and so I had to use a mixture of hand signals.

2. Admitting his mistake helped him to discover something about himself.

3. The cheetah can reach speeds in excess of 65 mph.

4. Properly using a seat-belt can prevent injuries in car accidents.

9. The Run-Away Thesaurus

1. The policeman's negligence allowed the criminal to get away.

2. The firefighter rescued the cat from the tree.

3. What is your name?

4. The lean high jumper easily made it over the bar.

5. That embarrassing person does nothing but wear me down.

6. Although an influential king, he behaved in a childish fashion.

7. It is difficult to behave properly when everyone else is so boisterous and rude.

7. Article Errors

1. The day before yesterday, we visited an historic landmark on the Thames River.

2. Where is the subway station? I saw it yesterday when we were looking for a hotel.

3. The time for rest is over. Now we must take an active part in saving the forests.

4. The sentence is correct.

6. Agreement Errors

1. A herd of pigs is often difficult to control if the pigs are not regularly fed.

2. The sentence is correct.

3. Shakespeare's understanding of dramatic action and his construction of plot are what make his later tragedies so incredibly powerful.

4. A hiker's worst nightmare is changing weather conditions.

5. The sentence is correct.

6. Each of the players is ready for the upcoming game, but only one is going to start.

5. The Typographical Error

1. "Haveyou" should be "Have you"
2. "buildng" is missing an "i"

3. "building" is repeated twice
4. the first sentence should end with a "."
5. "Th" is missing an "e"
6. "Takess" needs to lose an "s"
7. "he" should be "the"
8. "begin" should be "begins"
9. "the m" should be "them"
10. "the" is repeated twice before "tot"
11. "becames" should be "becomes"
12. the "." after "oh" should be a ","
13. "knocks" is repeated twice
14. there must be two spaces before "Cubist"
15. "thng" should be "thing"
16. "to" is repeated twice
17. "toelemental" needs a space
18. "gemetric" should be "geometric"
19. no "." after "planes"
20. "recontruct" should be "reconstruct"

3. Sentence Fragments

1. Even if she did come back after curfew, no one would have found out.

2. The honourable member was forced to concede this point.

3. It must take skill to be able to say that convincingly, without even batting an eyelash.

4. To create something with your bare hands is an amazing feeling.

2. Incomplete Thesis Statement

1. Because it is cost effective, practical, and a deterrent, capital punishment should be reinstated for those who commit first-degree murder.

2. Marital infidelity should be an impeachable offense for elected officials, because their actions might compromise national security and they should have to show strong moral leadership.

3. By teaching hand-eye coordination, the formation of strategical
    thinking, and cooperation, video games are a valuable learning tool
    for children.

4. The procedure for distributing parking passes at our university
    needs to be changed because black-market sales are encouraged
    and some students never get a pass.

5. Because it is more personal and less preoccupied with special
    effects, television is a far more interesting medium than film.